Stock Market Investing
for Beginners

Learn the Basics

of Stock Market Investing and

Strategies in 5 Days and

Learn It Well

By

Michael Ezeanaka

www.MichaelEzeanaka.com

Copyright ©2021

Disclaimer

This publication is designed to provide competent and reliable information regarding the subject matter covered. However, it is sold with the understanding that the author is not engaged in rendering investment or other professional advice. Laws and practices often vary from state to state and country to country and if investment or other expert assistance is required, the services of a professional should be sought. The author specifically disclaims any liability that is incurred from the use or application of the contents of this book.

Get Your PDF Chapter Summary Today

If you'll like to download a PDF Chapter Summary of this book, follow the below instructions:

1. Go to **https://michaelezeanaka.com**

2. Navigate to Free Stuff > Ebooks/Audiobooks > Stock Market Investing For Beginners (PDF Chapter Summery)

Other Investing Books by Michael Ezeanaka	
Book #	**Book Title**
1	Dividend Investing For Beginners – Learn The Basics Of Dividend Investing And Strategies In 5 Days And Learn It Well
2	Real Estate Investing For Beginners – Earn Passive Income With REITS, Tax Lien Certificates, Lease, Residential And Commercial Real Estate
Download the Audio Versions Along with The Complementary PDF Document for FREE from www.MichaelEzeanaka.com	

Table of Contents

Introduction

Mary was a single mother who didn't finish high school. She had a hard time finding employment, so to make ends meet, she decided to become a stay-in housemaid. She worked six days a week and almost sixteen hours a day. During her fifth year as a house helper, her employer gave her a $2000 bonus. She used that money to invest in the stock market. She met with a financial adviser, opened a stock investment account, and started investing. She continued to put in $120 a month to her investment account. After a few years, her $2000 investment grew to $120,000. She used a little bit of the money to start a small soap business and earned more.

Mary's story is not unique. She's only one of the millions of people who have made a lot of money investing in the stock market.

Stock market investment is a great option for you if you're looking for passive income options and the ability to earn money while you're asleep. Even so, you must know that not everyone wins big in the stock market. While a lot of people are getting richer through stock investment, a number of investors are losing money too. While some investors strike it rich, others lose all the money they invest. The stock market is not only an intimidating subject; it's also a bit of a slippery slope. This is the reason why you should have a deep understanding of how the stock market works before you even start investing.

You've given yourself a great advantage by getting a copy of this book. It contains basic stock market strategies that will help increase your chance of creating a profitable and sustainable stock portfolio. This book is written for first-time stock market investors, so it's easy to understand. It's basically *Stock Investing for Dummies*. It thoroughly explains seemingly intimidating concepts like stock trading, index investing, exchange-traded funds (ETFs), index fund investing, and penny stocks. It is your ultimate beginner guide to stock investing.

In this book, you'll discover:
- What the stock market is and how can you make money through it.
- What stocks are and why they exist.
- How the stock market works.
- The major players in the stock market.
- What an index is.
- The difference between a bull market and a bear market.
- The role that SEC and other regulators play in the stock market.
- How you can invest in the stock market.
- What a 401k plan is.
- What an IRA is and how it can help you achieve financial independence.
- Smart investment strategies that can help you earn bigger returns.
- How to pick the right stock to invest in.
- Factors to consider when choosing a stock.
- How to minimize unnecessary losses.
- The right companies to invest in.

- The stock research process.
- How to build a stock position.
- What a stockbroker is and how to pick the right one.
- How to read your broker trade confirmations.
- Types of trades you can place with your broker.
- How to manage and diversify your stock investment portfolio.

And much, much more!

What to Expect from This Book

As I've said before, this book has been specifically written for stock market beginners. Its goal is to explain complex financial and investment concepts in a simple way. Most stock market concepts are defined and explained in layman terms. You will also find a glossary, or "definition of terms section," towards the end of this book. This will help you understand intimidating stock market terms easily.

Chapter 1 covers basic information that you'll need to understand to master the art of stock market investment. In this chapter, you'll learn what the stock market is and how it works. You'll also learn:

- What stocks are and how they are created.
- Why the stock market is necessary.
- The difference between common and preferred stocks.
- The major stock market players.
- What an index is and how to use it.
- How you can make money in the stock market.
- The role of stock market regulators like the SEC.
- What a stock exchange is and why it exists.
- What a bear market is.
- What a bull market is.

You'll learn how to invest in the stock market in Chapter 2. This chapter will help you understand the basic investment plans available to you and how to choose the right one.

In that chapter, you'll learn:
- How to get started in the stock market.
- How to invest through a 401(k) plan.
- How to invest in an individual retirement plan or IRA.
- The difference between a 403(b) plan and a 401(k) plan.
- How to invest through a taxable brokerage account.
- How to invest through a direct stock purchase plan or dividend reinvestment plan.

Chapter 3 is about stock investment strategies, such as value investing, growth investing, dividend investing, day trading, and short selling.

Chapter 4 will help you decide how to choose the right stocks to invest in. In this chapter, you'll learn:
- How to set investment objectives.
- Factors you need to consider in choosing a stock.
- How to tell if a stock is overvalued.
- How to build a stock position.

Chapter 5 helps you understand your brokerage account statement. This chapter answers questions like:
- What is a brokerage account?
- What kinds of securities can a brokerage account hold?
- Is there a limit to the amount that you can deposit in a brokerage account?
- How many brokerage accounts can one have?
- What's the difference between a full-service and a discount broker?

In Chapter 6, you'll learn about the things that you can find in a brokerage trade confirmation, such as the name of the investment you have traded with the ticker symbol, the total shares bought or sold, the trade execution date, the cost or selling price per share, the commission you paid to the broker, the gross value of the transaction, and more.

Chapter 7 focuses on the types of trades you can place with your broker, such as market orders, limit orders, all-or-none orders, stop orders and stop-limit orders, buy to cover orders, trailing stop orders, day and GTC orders, and more.

Chapter 8 talks about the stock research process. You'll learn how to use macro-economic and micro-economic analysis to maximize your investment returns.

Chapter 9 helps you choose stocks for long-term investment. You'll learn the signs that a stock is good for long-term investment (e.g., a competitive advantage, a strong balance sheet, high returns of capital, etc. You'll also find high-quality stocks that you can explore.

Chapter 10 helps you understand the benefit of portfolio management strategies like diversification.

In addition to all of the above, there's a summary section at the end of each chapter to help you remember important points. Furthermore, the glossary (located at the end of this book) can help you understand complicated stock market concepts.

What Not to Expect from This Book

Gladys had read something about stock market investing online, and she was really excited. She opened an investment account and started investing money in stocks.

After *a few months*, Gladys was frustrated not to see significant returns on her investments. And so, she decided to give up.

Stock market investing isn't a "get rich quick" scheme. It takes time to grow your investments and achieve great wealth.

This book contains effective *long-term investment strategies* that you can use to become a successful investor. It's definitely not for those who are looking to double their investment in just a few months.

Stock market investing works a bit like gambling. When you're investing in a stock, you're betting on a specific outcome, and there are no guarantees. To increase your chance of winning, you have to rely on logic, sound investment strategies, and extensive research. This book will help you do that.

Finally, in order not to overwhelm beginner investors with too much information, this book will not cover technical analysis of stock charts.

Inspiration #1

"Buy a stock the way you would buy a house. Understand and like it such that you'd be content to own it in the absence of any market."
Warren Buffett

Chapter 1

Understanding the Stock Market

Warren Buffet is one of the wealthiest, most respected people in the world. And he became wealthy by leveraging the stock market. However, to become a wealthy investor like Warren, you must understand the stock market thoroughly—what it is and how it works.

This chapter will help you gain a basic understanding of what a stock is and how you could make money in the stock market.

What is a Stock?

A stock, or a share, is a piece of a company. The first-ever stock was created by the Dutch East India Company (Verenigde Oostindische Compagnie) in 1602 at the Amsterdam Stock Exchange.

Think of a business as a pizza, and the slices are its stocks or shares. When you purchase a stock from a company, you own a piece of that company. Let's say that ABC Company has 100,000 shares and you purchase 10,000 shares. This means that you own 10% of the company—its assets and revenues.

A stock is a form of security or a financial instrument that has monetary value and can be traded. This means that once you buy a stock, you are free to sell or trade it.

But why do stocks exist and how are they created? Well, companies create and issue shares when they need to raise money for expansion and business growth. Let's look at a story to illustrate this point. Joel started his small candy manufacturing company. Let's call it Candy Corp for the purposes of discussion. He started the company with only three thousand dollars. He bought a second-hand machine from another candy company that had recently closed shop.

He and his wife, Mara, produced a thousand candies and sold them online. After a year, the business grew, so they needed to hire two candy makers, an accountant, a delivery guy, and a customer service representative.

After five years, the three-thousand-dollar company grew. The demand for Candy Corp's products skyrocketed. Joel also wanted to produce more lollipops, jelly beans, and candy sticks, but he needed around $1 million to purchase new equipment, hire more people, expand his factory, meet the growing demand, and produce new candy types. Joel didn't have that kind of money. He also didn't want to borrow money from banks. So, he decided to sell a part of his company and go public. This process is called an Initial Public Offering or IPO, which we'll discuss in a while.

When an entrepreneur starts a business, it's classified as private. This means that his company has a limited number of shareholders (himself and angel investors like investment companies, family members, and friends). But, somewhere along the way, he would need more money to expand his business and cater to more customers. So, to avoid incurring debt and paying interest charges, he decides to sell a few pieces of his company. He can do this either privately (by raising money from existing shareholders) or publicly (by selling shares to new shareholders).

If he decides to sell his stocks privately, he can sell them to whomever he chooses to sell them to. He can sell it directly to a friend, a business acquaintance, or an angel investor. But, if he decides to sell his company shares faster, he would have to sell them to the public, and this isn't something that he can do himself. He has to go to an investment bank (let's call it IB). Based on the value of his company, he and IB determine the price of the stock, the number of shares that they should offer to the public, and the percentage of his business that he would have to give up.

Let's say that the entrepreneur's business is valued at $ 10 million and that he has to sell 10% of his company to raise additional capital of $1 million in an initial offering called IPO, which is done in a stock market.

An IPO is the first sale of the stock issued by a company to the public. This is the reason why people call it "going public." It's usually done at a stock market.

What is a Stock Market and How Does It Work?

A stock market is a place where people and companies issue, buy, and sell stocks. The stock market has two major purposes. The first is to help companies sell their stocks so they can raise capital for expansion. So, if a company issues 100,000 shares of stock for $10 per share, it could raise up to $1 million capital on its initial public offering.

The second purpose of the stock market is to give investors (the people who purchase stocks) the opportunity to earn from the profits of publicly traded companies. Let's say that an investor purchased a company stock for $10. When the value of the stock goes up to $20, he earns a profit of $10.

There are three types of stock markets:

1. Stock Exchanges

A stock exchange is a centralized location where people buy and sell shares. This market is essential to economic development, as it gives companies access to capital. It also gives the general public the opportunity to grow their money (through) stocks over time. There are two major stock exchanges in the United States:

The New York Stock Exchange

The New York Stock Exchange (NYSE) is the biggest and most popular stock market (in terms of capitalization) in the world. It is located on Wall Street, Manhattan, and it was founded on May 17, 1792. It was previously run by a private company, but it became a public organization in 2005. The parent company of the NYSE is called NYSE Euronext

Nasdaq

The National Association of Securities Dealers Automated Quotations (Nasdaq) is the second biggest stock exchange in the world (in terms of the capital it generates). It's located on Broadway Street, New York City and it was established in 1941. It's operated by a private company called Nasdaq Inc., which also operates a number of stock exchanges around the United States and in Stockholm, Copenhagen, Tallinn, Helsinki, Vilnius, Reykjavik, and Yerevan.

2. Electronic Communication Network

An ECN, or Electronic Communication Network, is a computerized network that facilitates the trade of securities and other financial products.

An ECN usually trades currencies and stocks. The first ECN was called Instinet and it was created in 1969. This financial market type is usually used by a number of Forex (foreign exchange) brokers. These brokers trade foreign currencies.

3. Over-The-Counter (OTC) Market

OTC markets are used to buy and sell bonds, currencies, derivatives, and structured products. These markets are also used to trade equities.

Primary vs. Secondary Markets

The stock market has two parts—the primary market and the secondary market. The primary market is where the stocks are created. The IPO, or initial public offering, is an example of a primary market transaction. When you buy a stock in a primary market, you're buying it directly from the company.

The secondary market, on the other hand, is where investors:
- Buy stocks from other investors and/or
- Sell shares they already own.

National exchanges such as NASDAQ and New York Stock Exchange are examples of secondary markets.

Why Do We Need a Stock Market?

The main goal of the stock market is to provide a structured and well-regulated exchange where investors can safely sell and buy stocks of publicly-traded corporations. It also provides companies the opportunity to generate capital by selling shares.

Major Stock Market Players

When you think of the stock market, you probably think of testosterone-loaded men in suits. You think of figurative wolves and people screaming on the phones. But these men in suits are only the tip of the iceberg. There are a number of stock market players, namely:

Investors

Investors are people who buy and sell stocks to earn a profit and grow their money. Investors earn money through dividends and capital appreciation. Let's say that an investor bought ten Company M shares for $10 each, so his total investment was $100. After six months, the price of Company M stocks increased to $15. So, if the investor decided to sell his shares, he would earn a profit (through capital appreciation) of $5.

There are two general types of investors—the "hands-on" investors and the "hands-off" investors.

Hands-off investors rely heavily on brokers. They don't pick the stocks they invest in. They usually invest in mutual funds, ETFs, and index funds.

Hands-on investors, on the other hand, personally handpick the stocks they invest in. They usually actively work with an experienced broker to build their investment portfolio.

Shareholders

Shareholders are investors who buy stocks from listed companies. They already own a small (sometimes big) part of certain companies.

There are two types of shareholders—common and preferred. Common shareholders, as the name suggests, own common stocks. They have voting rights. They can elect company officials, and they have a say in the development of company policies. But in case of asset liquidation, they're only paid after the creditors and preferred stockholders get their share.

Preferred shareholders, on the other hand, own preferred stocks. They do not have voting rights, but, they rank higher than the common shareholders. In the case of asset liquidation, preferred shareholders are paid before common stockholders get their share.

Listed Companies

Companies listed on stock exchanges are also called "issuers." They sell their shares in the stock market to raise money for expansion. They go through a process called an Initial Public Offering, or IPO.

Stockbrokers

A stockbroker is a third-party stock market participant that trades stocks and other securities on behalf of clients or investors. This could be an individual or someone from a brokerage firm.

Representatives of these stockbrokers meet daily at a specific time on the stock exchange trading floor where they buy, sell, and execute orders on behalf of their clients.

There are two main types of stockbrokers:
- *Traditional* –They take orders from their clients in person or via phone.
- *Online* – They do not interact with their clients. They just take the order from their clients through an online platform.

Venture Capitalists

Venture capitalists are companies (or people) who invest in early-stage companies. They often invest between one million to one hundred million dollars—sometimes even more. They also usually take a board seat in the company they invest in.

Investment Bank or Underwriter

An investment bank (or underwriter) is an organization that manages the IPO process.
Investment banks draft the necessary documents, find investors, and perform the company valuation. They also conduct roadshows to encourage people to invest in companies they're representing.
These investment banks usually charge between 2% and 7% of the total amount of money they raised during the IPO. There are many Wall Street investment banks, such as JP Morgan, Morgan Stanley, and Goldman Sachs.

Floor Trader

A floor trader is a member of a stock exchange who trades on the floor for his own account.

Floor Broker

A floor broker executes trades on the exchange floor on behalf of clients. He executes orders placed by clients.

Clearing House

A clearinghouse is a financial institution that facilitates the exchange of securities and payments. Its goal is to make sure that the exchange participants honor their trade settlement obligations.
The clearinghouse settles member's trade accounts and collects money. It also oversees the delivery of stocks and generates trading data.

Let's say that James sells fifty Company X shares for $2,500 on a stock exchange. Diana buys fifty Company X shares for $2,500.

Diana doesn't have to pay James directly for the stocks she purchased. The stock exchange's clearinghouse collects $2,500 from Diana's trade account and transfers it to James's account.

Analysts

Analysts examine certain stocks to predict future revenues, earnings, and prices.

Online Investors

These investors just set up an online account and trade from home.

Financial Advisors

These people manage other people's money.

Financial Authors

These people do market analysis and publish stock trading theories to help people become intelligent investors.

How Can You Make Money Out of Your Stock Investment

People invest in the stock market to make more money. You can earn money from stock investment in two ways:

Capital Appreciation

You may have already heard the motto of every stockbroker on Wall Street: "Buy low, sell high."
Let's say that you bought a stock for $150 (buying price). Then, two years later, you decided to sell the stock, which is now valued at $300 (selling price). This means that you made a profit of $150. The positive difference between the buying and the selling price is called capital appreciation. This is the easiest way to earn money from the stock market.

Dividends

When a company earns a profit, it can do two things: it can use the money to expand or it can distribute the profit to its shareholders. Some companies do both, distributing a portion of the profits to the shareholders and using the remaining money for expansion. The profits distributed among the stockholders are called "dividends."

A dividend is a portion of the profit distributed to a specific class of stockholders decided by the board of directors.

Dividends are normally distributed on a "per-share" basis. Let's say that you have purchased 200 shares of Company Z, which is valued at $100 each. So, your total investment is valued at $20,000 (200 x 100).

Let's say that Company Z is really doing well this year and decides to pay a dividend of $20 per share. This means that you'll get a payout of $4000 (200 shares x $20 per share) and a dividend yield of 20% (the dividend divided by the price of the stock).

You must remember that not all stocks come with regular dividend payments. In fact, not all companies distribute dividends to their shareholders. And when they do, companies can choose which class of stockholders they want to distribute it to (common or preferred shareholders, which we'll discuss shortly).

Growing companies are less likely to give out dividends because they'll most likely reinvest their profits to provide "fuel" for further expansion. Large companies, on the other hand, don't need to expand, so they opt to give out dividends to their shareholders on a regular basis.

Common vs Preferred Stocks

Both common and preferred stocks represent ownership of a company. Both are tools that investors can use to earn money in the long run. They have a lot of similarities, but they also have a number of differences.

Common Stocks

Common stocks, as the name suggests, are more common than preferred ones. These stocks are generally cheaper and riskier too.

Common stock is a type of security that represents ownership of a part of a company. Common stockholders have voting rights (depending on the number of shares they hold). They can vote on corporate policies and possible mergers. They can also elect board directors.

Aside from voting rights, investing in a common stock also comes with a lot of other benefits. For one, it has a higher yield than bonds and other investment products. It also comes with restricted legal liability. This means that the shareholders are not liable when the company is sued. It's also a highly liquid investment. This means that it's easy to purchase and sell.

The downside of being a common stockholder is that they are at the bottom of the company ownership structure. This means that if a company goes bankrupt and decides to liquidate its assets and properties, common shareholders have the right to the company equity only after creditors, bondholders, and preferred stockholders are paid.

Right to Company Assets in the Event of Liquidation

1st Priority	Creditors/Bond Holders
2nd Priority	Preferred Stockholders
3rd priority	Common Stockholders

If you're a common stockholder, there's no guarantee that you'll get paid when the company goes bankrupt. This is the reason why it's risky.

Preferred Stocks

Preferred stocks are like a hybrid of bonds and stocks. They have features of both a stock and a bond.

Preferred stocks have higher dividend rates. This means that they have higher returns. They're also less risky than common stocks. Why? Well, in case the company decides to liquidate its assets and properties, preferred stockholders get paid before common shareholders.

Like the common stock, a preferred stock also represents ownership of a company. But, it's different from the common share in the sense that preferred stockholders are paid a fixed dividend at regular intervals (e.g., annually, quarter).

Let's say that Company X issues new preferred stocks at $50 each. Then, they agreed to pay a dividend yield of $2 a year. This means that this stock has a dividend yield of 4% (annual dividend ($2) divided by the price of the stock ($50). This is a bit similar to how a bond works.

The downside of investing in preferred stocks is that you do not have voting rights. This means that you do not have a say regarding company policies. You also can't elect board members. Moreover, when a company faces financial problems, the company can cut dividend payments to preferred stockholders.

Preferred stocks also have a low trading volume. This means that you can't easily expand your preferred stock portfolio.

There are also a lot of factors that can decrease the value of a preferred stock, such as the interest rate. Let's say that your preferred stock has an annual yield of 4%. When the interest rate rises to 7%, a lot of preferred stockholders may opt to sell their share and reinvest their money in items that pay higher dividends. This could drive the price of the preferred stock lower.

Powerful investors like Warren Buffet have a huge portfolio of preferred stocks. But, before you put your eggs in the preferred stock basket, you must be aware that only a few companies issue preferred stocks. These companies are usually in the financial sector—banks, lending companies, insurance outfits, etc. You should know this because investing in the financial industry is a bit risky, as these companies usually have thin profit margins.

Why Do Stock Prices Fluctuate?

The stock market works like an auction house. This means that the price of a stock is basically based on the perceived value of the market players.

The price of a company's stock can change based on a lot of market forces, including the "law of supply and demand." This means that a high-demand stock is more expensive than a low-demand stock.

Let's take Berkshire Hathaway as an example. Its share is currently valued at $115,000 (more or less), the most expensive in the world.

This company is a multinational conglomerate that wholly owns Duracell, Dairy Queen, NetJets, Fruit of the Loom, Helzberg Diamonds, and GEICO. It also owns a part of Apple, Bank of America, Kraft Heinz Company, American Express, Pilot Flying J, and Coca-Cola.

But why is it so expensive? Its supply is too low because current stockholders do not sell their share, and yet a lot of people want a share of the pie. It's expensive because the supply is a lot less than the demand. Warren Buffet also keeps the prices high to keep short-term investors from causing price volatility.

Aside from the "law of supply and demand," there are other factors that affect a stock's price, including future estimated earnings, mergers, acquisitions, accounting errors, employee layoffs, corporate scandals, and many more.

Let's say that there are two pasta companies, A and B. Company A is using a traditional pasta recipe. It's stable and established, so its stock is sold at $100 each.

Company B, on the other hand, uses avocado sauce. It's interesting but a bit too inventive, so its stock is sold at a lower price of $50.

Let's say that popular chefs tasted Company B's pasta and thought that it was the best culinary invention next to bread. For this reason, its stock price increased to $100.

Now, let's say that experts discover that Company A's pasta has an ingredient that can cause cancer. Do you think that its stock price would still be $100? Hell, no! This scandal can significantly reduce its stock price. No one would want to invest in Company A anymore.

7 Economic Forces That Affect Stock Prices:

1. Economic Policy Changes

A new government leader may enforce new policies, and this can heavily affect stock prices. Policy changes can either positively or negatively impact prices.

For example, if there's a policy that imposes a sugar tax on soft drinks, the stock prices of soda companies will go down. The stock price of tobacco companies will go up when the government decides to deregulate the cigarette producers.

2. Interest Rates

A country's central bank can increase or decrease interest rates to either stimulate or stabilize its economy. This process is called "monetary policy," and it can affect stock prices.

Let's say that Company K decided to borrow money from the bank for expansion. At that moment, the interest rate was really high, so the company's debt was a bit costly. This decreased Company K's profits and dividend payments. This also decreased the company's stock price.

3. Predictions of Financial Analysts

If economists and financial experts think that the economy is going to expand soon, stock prices tend to rise. Investors buy more stocks, as they anticipate higher stock prices and future profits.
When economists predict a possible economic recession, investors panic and end up selling their stocks to invest in safe havens (e.g., treasury bills, gold, etc.). This drives stock prices down.

4. Inflation

Inflation is the increase in the prices of consumer products. This usually reduces profits as it increases costs and also leads to higher interest rates. The Central Bank may temporarily increase the interest rates in order to make money more expensive to borrow and hence control its supply in the economy. This helps to keep inflation under control, as there's less money being spent to acquire products/assets—classic supply and demand. It can also decrease stock prices.

When inflation increases, purchasing power declines, and each dollar can buy fewer goods and services. For investors interested in income-generating stocks, or stocks that pay dividends, the impact of high inflation makes these stocks less attractive than during low inflation, since dividends generally fail to keep up with inflation levels.

5. Deflation

Deflation is the complete opposite of inflation. When the prices go down, revenues and profits decrease. This can decrease the stock prices, and investors may end up selling their shares.

6. Political Issues and Crime

Political instability often leads to economic instability. For example, a massive act of terrorism such as the 9/11 attacks can decrease economic activities and also reduce stock prices as investors sell their shares to invest in safe havens like gold.

7. Natural Disasters

Natural disasters are scary and difficult to predict. They can destroy lives and economies. They can dampen economic growth and decrease stock prices.

If you want to be a successful investor, you must examine these factors thoroughly.

What a Stock Exchange Is and Why It's Important.

A stock exchange is an organized marketplace where securities such as stocks are traded. Huge amounts of money are moved back and forth in the stock market. More than fifty trillion dollars are traded every year in stock exchanges. This is more than the sum of the value of all the products and services of all world economies.

There are two major stock exchanges in the United States, including:

New York Stock Exchange (NYSE)

The New York Stock Exchange (NYSE) is located on Wall Street, Manhattan. It was founded on May 17, 1792, and it's the biggest stock exchange in the world in terms of the capital it generates.

Stocks are traded in NYSE in two ways: through brokers and electronic systems. Brokers (who represent investors) actively buy and sell stocks in this stock exchange.

National Association of Securities Dealers Automated Quotations (NASDAQ)

National Association of Securities Dealers Automated Quotations (Nasdaq) is the second-largest stock exchange in the world in terms of the capital it generates. It is located on Broadway in New York. It is operated by Nasdaq Inc., which also owns stock exchanges in various cities in the world, including Stockholm, Copenhagen, Vilnius, Riga, Tallinn, Helsinki, Reykjavik, and Yerevan.

What Is an Index?

Like a store, the stock market has different products with varying values and prices. But, how do you know which one to invest in? How do you make the most out of your investment? Well, you must be familiar with different tools, terms, and concepts that can help you make a wise, informed stock investment decision.

To see how a stock market is performing, many investors look at stock indices. An index is a small sample of stocks that are thought to represent a specific sector or the market in general.

You see, there's no way that one can monitor the performance and the value of all the shares in the stock market. This is the reason why financial analysts just pull a sample of stocks from different industries such as manufacturing, mining, fashion, commodities, real estate, healthcare, and many more. So, when you see a business reporter announce that the market is up by 3%, he's actually referring to an index, or a small sample of stocks.

Indices are used to measure change. They are indicators of the financial health of specific stock markets and industries.

To illustrate this point, let's say that you have invested in a few healthcare companies, but, the IXHC (Nasdaq Health Care Index) is continuously decreasing. This information helps you make a wise financial decision. Maybe it's time to reassess your investments and look for other industries to invest in.

There are many types of indices around the globe, but here's a list of the most popular and widely used indices:

The Standard & Poor's 500 (S&P 500)

This index reflects the average market value (price of share x the number of outstanding or held shares) of five hundred "most held" stocks from different industries. These stocks are held, meaning they are already owned. The companies included in the S&P sample are chosen based on a number of factors, including their market size and how much they represent their industry.

The S&P 500 measures the performance of large-cap and established companies from different industries, such as Abbott Laboratories (health care), Adobe Systems (information technology), Colgate-Palmolive (consumer products), Facebook (communications), Microsoft (information technology), Tiffany & Co (discretionary consumer products), and Wal-Mart (consumer staples).

Dow Jones Industrial Average (DJIA)

The Dow Jones Industrial Average (DJIA) is the oldest and, perhaps, the most popular stock market index. It was created in 1885 as DJA and it was renamed DJIA on May 26, 1896.

This index takes the sum of the thirty largest stocks in the New York Stock Exchange & NASDAQ, and divides it by a divisor. The divisor is used to ensure that a one-point move in a lower-priced component will have the identical effect on DJIA as does a one-point move in a higher-priced component. The current divisor can be found in the *Wall Street Journal* and is: **0.14748071991788**.

DJIA = Sum (Component Stock Prices)/Dow Divisor

The stocks included in DJIA are so heavily traded, they are great indicators of the overall health of the stock market.

Nasdaq Composite Index

The Nasdaq Composite Index measures over three thousand stocks. It used to exclusively measure tech stocks such as Adobe and Google, but it has added stocks from different industries over the last few years.

The Difference between a Bear and a Bull Market

As previously mentioned, the stock market works a lot like an auction house. The prices of the stocks are driven by perception. There are times when public confidence is really high and optimistic, which results in investors buying more stocks. There are also times when the investors become so pessimistic that they ended up selling most of their shares. These occurrences are respectively called "bull" and "bear" markets.

Bear Market

No, we're not talking about the cute, huge, and fluffy mammals. In finance, a bear is a pessimistic investor, who believes that the stock market is going downward.

A bear market is a condition when a stock's value declines by at least 20% for a long period of time (at least two months) because of the investors' pessimism. When this happens, a lot of investors would opt to sell their stocks, and this would further fuel the negativity. This phenomenon usually lasts about thirteen months.

There are a lot of factors that push stocks into a bear market, including:

Forecasted Recession

A recession is a condition where there's a decrease in economic activity for a long period of time. This means that there's a decrease in major economic indicators, such as GDP (gross domestic product), manufacturing, disposable income, and employment.

When a country has a sluggish economy for a long period of time, economists may forecast a recession. This could push investors to sell their securities and drive the prices lower.

Commodity Price Increase

Commodities are investment pieces that include a wide array of industrial and edible products such as wheat, oil, steel, cotton, gold, coffee, sugar, cocoa, corn, live cattle, and gasoline. An increase in commodity prices can lead to inflation. This could negatively impact the stock market and could push it to the bear market territory.

Aggressive Central Bank

Each economy (country) has a central bank. This bank controls the country's money supply and interest rates.

But sometimes, a central bank can get aggressive in increasing the interest rates to prevent inflation. When this happens, people end up selling their stocks in favor of *high-interest* investments, such as a certificate of deposit, high-interest savings, money market funds, and U.S. savings bonds.

This could decrease the prices of stocks and could encourage investors to sell their shares to prevent losses and maximize their gains.

Extreme Valuations of Stocks

Overvaluation of stocks (vis-à-vis their earnings and intrinsic value) can lead to a bear market condition as exemplified by the economic state of the United States in 2001/2002.

As previously mentioned, a bear market usually lasts for thirteen months. Longer periods of a bear market can lead to a stock market crash. This happened in 1973 when the stock market remained depressed for more than ten years.

Is there a way to still make money out of stocks during a bear market period? Yes, you can use a technique that Warren Buffet uses called "value investing." This means that you should not look at the price of the stock, but rather, its intrinsic value (its profits, earnings, and assets). We will discuss this investing technique later on in the book.

Furthermore, extremely savvy investors can also benefit from stock market crashes by shorting the right stocks (i.e., stocks that are *most likely* to underperform, especially in bear market conditions).

Bull Market

A Bull Market is a condition in which the stock markets are so high that investors are aggressively buying stocks, acting like bulls. This period could last for months or even years.

A bull market is characterized by very high investor confidence and optimism. It happens when the stock prices increase by 20% for a long period of time (usually two months).

This phenomenon is difficult to predict, so financial analysts usually recognize a bull market after it has happened. The most famous bull market happened in 2003 and ended in 2007.

There are many factors that push the stock market into the "bull" territory, including an increase in GDP (gross domestic product) and a decrease in the unemployment rate.

During a bull market period, the demand for stocks surpasses its supply, causing the stock prices to rise.

Bear Market Vs. Bull Market	
The demand for stocks is lower than its supply – people would rather sell than buy stocks.	The stock demand is higher than its supply – many people are willing to buy stocks, but only a few wants to sell.
Investor confidence is low.	Investors are optimistic and willing to buy more stocks.
The economy is weak and unemployment rates are high.	The economy is strong, creating more jobs and increasing employment rates.

What is SEC and Its Role in the Stock Market

The stock market is a jungle filled with naïve beginners, greedy veterans, and glib stockbrokers. If it's not regulated, the greedy and deceptive predators could easily prey on uninformed investors. This is the reason why stock markets have regulators.

The SEC or the Securities Exchange Commission is a government agency that regulates the buying and selling of securities like bonds and stocks to protect investors from fraud and scams. It was created in 1934, making it the first federal stock market regulator. It regulates the New York Stock Exchange (NYSE) and the NASDAQ Stock Exchange.

The SEC oversees the companies, individuals, and organizations in the stock markets, including brokers, dealers, investors, securities exchanges, financial advisors, and various investment funds.

This government body provides investors access to important documents, such as financial reports and registration statements.

The United States SEC also uses different laws to accomplish its tasks. These include the Securities Act of 1933, the Trust Indenture Act of 1939, the Securities Exchange Act of 1934, the Investment Company Act (1940), the Investment Advisers Act (1940), the Sarbanes-Oxley Act (2002), the Jumpstart Our Business Startups (JOBS) Act of 2012, and the Dodd-Frank Wall Street Reform and Consumer Protection Act of 2010.

The SEC has five divisions, including:

- **Division of Trading and Markets** – This division creates and maintains standards to keep the stock markets orderly, efficient, and fair.

- **Division of Economic and Risk Analysis** – This division was created in 2009, and it uses data analytics to proactively identify market risks and violations of the securities law. This department is involved in various activities in the SEC, including policy-making, examination, and enforcement.

- **Division of Enforcement** – This department implements security laws and investigates violations.

- **Division of Investment Management** – As the name suggests, this department regulates several stock market players, such as investment companies and registered investment advisors.

- **Division of Corporate Finance** – This department ensures that investors have access to documents that can help them make sound investment decisions.

However, the SEC is not the only agency that regulates the US stock market. The Financial Industry Regulatory Authority (FINRA) is a private company that acts as an SRO or self-regulatory organization.

FINRA was established in 1939, and its goal is to make sure that the stock market operates honestly, openly, and fairly. It oversees all securities licensing requirements and processes. It administers exams needed to become a licensed financial adviser. It also enforces high ethical standards among stock market players to ensure that investors are protected.

Chapter 1 Summary

Below are some summary points from Chapter 1.

- Stock market investment is a technique used by investors like Warren Buffet to grow their money and accumulate wealth.

- Some people earn a lot of money from the stock market while others end up losing huge amounts of money. This is the reason why you must be well-informed before you start investing your money.

- A stock is a part of a company. It is a form of security. If a business is a pizza, a stock is a slice of the pizza.

- Companies create and issue stocks to raise additional capital for expansion.

- When a company decides to sell stocks, it goes through a process called an Initial Public Offering (IPO). This process is also called "going public."

- A stock market is a place where stocks are traded.

- The stock market has two parts: the primary market and the secondary market.

- The primary market is where the stocks are created. The secondary market is where investors buy previously-traded stocks and sell stocks they already own.

- There are three types of stock markets, including stock exchanges, electronic communication networks (ECNs), and over-the-counter (OTC) markets.

- The stock markets have various players, including corporations, investors, brokers, online investors, financial authors, and financial advisors.

- There are two ways that you can make money out of your stock investment: dividends and capital appreciation.

- A dividend is a profit distributed among shareholders.

- Capital appreciation is the positive difference between a stock's buying price and its selling price. It is a form of investor profit.

- Common stock represents ownership of a company. Common stockholders have voting rights. This means that they have a say in how company policies are shaped, and they can elect board members as well. However, they are at the bottom of the payout hierarchy. This means that if the company assets are liquidated, they only get paid after the preferred stockholders get paid.

- A preferred stock acts like a bond. It is more expensive than common stocks and usually comes with dividends. When the company assets are sold, preferred stockholders get their share after creditors and bond-holders are paid.

- Stock prices are affected by many factors, including the law of supply and demand, company news, forecasts, scandals, mergers, and acquisitions.

- An index is a small sample of stocks of companies that are so big that they represent the overall health of the industry they belong to.

- A bear market is a condition when investors are so pessimistic that they end up selling their stocks. This drives down the stock prices.

- A bull market is a condition when investors are optimistic, so they want to invest in stocks.

- The SEC is a stock market regulator that protects investors from fraud and scams.

In the next chapter, we'll discuss how you can invest in stocks.

Inspiration #2

"It's far better to buy a wonderful company at a fair price than a fair company at a wonderful price."
Warren Buffer

Chapter 2

Getting Started: How to Invest in Stocks

Eden has been working in an advertising agency for fifteen years. She's earning good money, but she's tired and wants to retire early. She always wanted to invest in stocks but didn't know how.

Much like Eden, many of us want to invest in the stock market, but we just don't know what to do or how to get started.

Investing in the stock market is not as hard as you think. Here are a few steps that you need to follow to get started:

Step 1: Understand the Difference between Stocks and Stock Mutual Funds

Many people think that stock market investing is a complicated animal. Well, that's not really the case. You just need to understand the two investment types:

Exchange-Traded Funds (ETF), or Stock Mutual Funds

Stock mutual funds allow you to buy small pieces of different stocks in one transaction.
ETFs and Index Funds are stock mutual funds that allow you to track an index and replicate it. For example, the S&P's 500 fund replicates the "Standard & Poor's 500" index.

So, if you decide to invest a little bit of your money in an "S&P's 500" fund, you'll own a little piece of all the companies in it (the size of that piece depends on your investment budget). You can't choose which stock(s) to invest in.

The upside of investing in ETFs is that they're cheaper. It's also *a great way to diversify your stock investments without spending a fortune.* However, the downside of this investment type is that it doesn't allow you to choose specific stocks to invest in. This brings us to the second investment type.

Individual Stocks

You need to invest in individual stocks if you're after a particular company. For example, if you really want a piece of Facebook, you need to buy a few FB stocks on Nasdaq.
You can also build a diversified portfolio out of several individual stocks, but you'd need to have a lot of money to do this.

Step 2: Identify Your Investing Style

You can invest in the stock market in a number of ways. You can invest in employer-sponsored accounts, such as the 401(k) plan; you can directly purchase stocks; or you can ask a financial advisor to manage your investments.

It's best to invest in a 401k Plan if you're on a budget and you're still working. But, if you're planning to invest a huge amount of money in the stock market, it's best to open a brokerage account or ask a professional money manager to manage your investment.

If you're not really a "hands-on" investor, it's best to invest in mutual funds, index funds, or ETFs. But, if you want to choose stocks yourself, then opening a brokerage account is the best option for you.

Step 3: Set a Budget

Before you start investing money in stocks, you must set a budget. How much money are you willing to invest? Remember that the amount of money you need depends on how much the shares cost. Some stocks cost a few dollars, while some shares can cost thousands of dollars.

Step 4: Open a Stock Investment Account

You need an investment account in order to invest in stocks. You can open a 401(k) account through your employer or you could open an IRA (individual retirement account). You can also open a brokerage account if you're more of a "hands-on" investor. We will discuss the different types of stock investment accounts in the latter part of this chapter.

As mentioned earlier, you can open an investment account with your employer. But, if you decide to open a brokerage account, you should consider the following factors:

Account Minimum

A lot of brokerage firms require a minimum initial investment of $500 or more. If you plan to initially invest just a few hundred dollars on the stock market, you should choose brokers that do not require minimum investments, such as Merrill Edge, TD Ameritrade, and Ally Invest.

Commissions

If you decide to invest in individual stocks, you'll have to pay for each trade commission (usually between 4 to 7 dollars). You should choose a broker with minimal trade commission rates, especially if you're a beginner.

Trading Style

If you're new to stock market investment, you probably don't need advanced trading platforms, but you may want to choose a brokerage firm that offers educational tools like tutorials, videos, and even seminars.

High-volume traders, on the other hand, need state-of-the-art trading platforms and analysis tools.

Account Fees

Most brokerage firms charge account fees such as annual fees, transfer fees, trading platform subscriptions, research fees, market data payments, and inactivity fees. It's best to choose a firm that offers free market data and research services and charges minimal account fees.

Step 5: Start Investing

Once you've opened an account, you can start investing, using different strategies, such as value investing, growth investing, income investing, socially responsible investing, diversification, and more. We'll discuss these strategies later on in this book.

401(k) Plan

The 401k plan is a retirement plan that companies offer to their employees as part of the benefits package. It is one of the most common retirement savings accounts. It was created in 1978 through the section 401(k) of the Internal Revenue Code. That's why it's called the 401(k) plan.

The best thing about the 401k plan is that it allows you to save on tax payments. It also allows you to take advantage of your employer's retirement contribution through the "employee matching gift" program. This program is usually offered as an incentive to prevent attrition and encourage employees to stay with the company for a long period of time.

Here's how it works. Let's say that you work in a tech company that sponsors 401k plans and you earn $150,000 a year before taxes. You agree to put 6% of your income, which sums up to $9000. This contribution is tax-deferred. This means that you don't have to pay taxes for your contribution until you retire (you'll be in a lower tax bracket when that time comes). This means that your taxable income at the moment is $141,000 (your annual income minus your annual contribution).

As a part of the matching gift program, your employer agrees to match $0.50 for every dollar you put into your 401(k) plan. So, the company puts an extra $4500 ($9000 x 0.50 cents). This means that your total contribution is $13,500 a year. See the computation below.

Employee contribution ($9,000)

+

Employer contribution ($4,000)

Total Annual 401(k) contribution ($13,500)

What Happens to Your 401(k) Contribution?

The money invested in your 401(k) account is usually invested in stocks, bonds, and mutual funds. When you sign up for this program, you'll be provided with a list of stocks that you can invest in. Review these stocks carefully.

You must consider your age when choosing the right stocks to invest in. If you're still in your twenties, it's okay to take a little risk. You can invest in volatile tech stocks like Netflix, Facebook, and Amazon.

But if you're already in your late thirties, forties, or fifties, it's best to go with more stable companies like Hormel Foods Corporation, Costco Wholesale, Cigna, and American Waterworks.

When you decide to quit your job, you can move your 401(k) plan to an IRA (individual retirement account). You can also roll over your existing plan to your new company's 401(k) plan, but you have to take note that not all companies accept retirement plan rollovers, so it's best to check with your new employer.

You can withdraw your 401(k) money even before you reach your retirement age, but the IRS (Internal Revenue Service) will have to collect a 10% early withdrawal penalty. This may not seem much if you saved $3000. But, if you already saved a million dollars, you'll have to pay a bigger penalty.

How to Invest in 401(k) Plan

As previously mentioned, the 401(k) plan is employee-sponsored. This means that you have to do it through your employer.

Here's how you can invest in the 401(k) plan:
- When you get hired, choose to be part of your company's 401(k) program.
- Decide how much of your income you want to go to your 401(k) plan.
- Choose the stocks that you want to invest in.
- Review your application, and submit it to your employer.

At this point, you don't have to do anything else. Your employer will automatically deduct your contribution from your salary. Your company also manages your investment fund, so you don't have to worry about anything.

401(k) Plan vs 403(B) Plan

Like the 401(k), the 403(b) is a retirement plan set up by an employer. The main difference is that 401(k) plans are offered by private and for-profit employers, while 403(b) plans are offered by non-profit employers, such as the government or non-profit schools.

If you work as a graphic designer in an advertising agency, you'll have the option to invest in a 401(k) retirement plan, but, if you work for a government agency, your employer will most likely offer a 403(b) retirement plan.

401(k) vs. 403(b)	
401 (K)	**403 (B)**
Retirement plan offered by private for profit companies	Retirement plan offered by non-profit organizations, such as religious groups, government organizations, and non-profit schools.
Higher administrative costs	Lower administrative costs
Has a maximum contribution limit	Has a maximum contribution limit
Has limited investment options usually selected by your employer or a financial management company	Account holders can invest in a wide variety of annuities and mutual funds
Has an employer matching program	Has an employing matching program

Pros and Cons of the 401(k) Plan

The biggest advantage of the 401(k) plan is that it comes with matching funds. So, you'll get a lot more money than you put in. Let's say, you committed to saving $7,000 a year, and your company matches your contribution and also deposits $7,000 to your account each year. This means that you'll have a total annual savings/investment of $14,000. Amazing, right?

The 401(k) plan is also hassle-free. You don't have to manage your investment account. It has high contribution limits, and it's protected by the ERISA, or the Employee Retirement Income Security Act of 1974.

But, the downside of the 401(k) plan is that it has limited investment options. This means that you can only invest in specific stocks and bonds.

IRA

Joy was a hard worker. Although she didn't finish high school, she found a stable job. She worked as a warehouse manager for thirty long years. The pay was good, but she ended up spending everything she had made. When she finally retired, she only had $10,000 in savings, which only covered a few months of her living expenses. Her pension benefits simply weren't enough.

Unfortunately, Joy's story is not unique. More and more retirees are broke. To avoid ending up like Joy, it's best to invest in an IRA.

An IRA, or individual retirement account, is a tax-advantaged investment and a savings account that allows you to save for retirement.

There are different types of IRAs—namely, traditional IRAs, Roth IRAs, Simple IRAs, Spousal IRAs, nondeductible IRAs, SEP IRAs, and self-directed IRAs.

Traditional IRA

A traditional IRA is a tax-deferred retirement savings and investment account. It is the most popular retirement plan. As the traditional IRA is tax-deferred, your contribution is not taxed now, but it's taxed when you withdraw the money from your account. This investment type is great for people who will be placed in a lower income tax bracket when they retire.

So, let's say that you're single and you earn $210,000 per year. Your tax is 35% and your yearly retirement savings is $6,500 per year. This means that you have to pay a tax of $2,275 per year for your investment. That's too much, right.

Now, if you place your money in a traditional IRA account, you won't have to pay taxes for your retirement plan. You'll pay when you retire and by that time, your tax is 15%. This means that instead of paying $2,275 annual tax for your investment, you'll only have to pay $975. This will save you 57% more money or around $1,300 per year!

Here are the key features of traditional IRA:

- It's a tax-deferred account. This means that you only have to pay taxes for your investment plan upon withdrawal.
- It has bankruptcy protection. This means that your creditors can't go after your IRA.
- Your beneficiaries can inherit your IRA funds in case of death.
- You can set up an IRA even if you have another retirement plan.
- You can convert your 401(k) plan into a traditional IRA when you decide to leave your employer.
- You can invest your savings into stocks, mutual funds, and other securities.
- Traditional IRA has a 10% early withdrawal penalty, except in some cases, such as:
  - ➢ Death (when this happens, the beneficiaries can withdraw the funds)

➢ Disability
➢ Back taxes
➢ Conversion of Traditional IRA to another retirement plan, such as Roth IRA
➢ IRS civil suit
➢ Creditor access
➢ Medical expenses
➢ Higher education payments

Investing in a Traditional IRA

Step 1 – Choose a brokerage company.

Decide what your investing style is. If you're a hands-off investor, you can invest via a robo-advisor, an online/digital financial advisor that manages your investments with minimal human intervention. Robo-advisors are usually efficient, and they're cheaper than regular brokerage firms.

If you're more of a hands-on investor, you should choose a broker that has low account and commission fees. Most importantly, choose a broker with a good reputation. You don't want to get scammed and lose all your hard-earned money.

Step 2 – Open an account.

Opening a traditional IRA account is not as hard as you think. All you need to do is fill out some forms. You would need to provide personal details, such as your date of birth, social security number or SSN, employment data, and contact information.

Step 3 – Start depositing money into your account.

You can transfer money from your bank account into your traditional IRA. You will need your account number and bank routing number if you're transferring funds for the first time. You can also roll over a 401(k) plan from your former employer into your IRA.

Step 4 – Choose your investments.

When you decide to invest via a robo-advisor, you don't get to choose your investments. On the other hand, if you decide to invest through a broker, you'll have to choose which stocks or ETFs that you want to invest in.

Roth IRA

Like the traditional IRA, the Roth IRA is a tax-advantaged retirement investment plan. It's named after Senator William Roth of Delaware.

A Roth IRA is a lot like the traditional IRA in many ways, but, the major difference is that *it's tax-free (not tax-deferred).* You'll have to pay the tax annually, but all the taxes paid will be refunded once you withdraw your investment.

Here's how it works. Let's say that you decide to contribute $5,500 per year (for 20 years) and you have a tax rate of 10%. You'll get a tax deduction of $550 per year for 20 years which sums to $11,000. Once you retire, you'll receive a tax refund of $11,000. Amazing, right?

Anyone with taxable income can open a Roth IRA. Here are the top features of this investment plan:
- You can contribute a maximum of $5,500 a year.
- It's tax-free, but you'll still get a tax deduction every month. The taxes paid will be refunded when you retire.
- You can open multiple IRAs.
- You can withdraw your Roth IRA funds without paying taxes or penalties five years after opening the account, but, it's only tax-free and penalty-free in certain cases such as:
  - Disability
  - IRA owner's death
  - Money was used for medical expenses
  - Money was used to pay for insurance premiums
  - The saved money was used to pay back taxes
  - The fund was used for a first-time home purchase
  - The IRA fund was used to pay for higher education

Roth IRA is more flexible than the traditional IRA. Plus, you can withdraw it without any penalty in the event that you suffer an illness, become disabled, or need to purchase your first home. Plus, it's something that you can pass on to your heirs.

But, there's one drawback. Single people who have a modified adjusted gross income (MAGI) of more than $137,000 a year or married couple (filing jointly) with an annual MAGI of more than $203,000 cannot open a Roth IRA account (as of January, 2019).

How to Get Started with a Roth IRA

Step 1 – Find out if you're eligible to open a Roth IRA.

As previously mentioned, not everyone is qualified to open a Roth IRA. If you're single, head of the family, and you earn more than $135,000, you're not allowed to open a Roth IRA. So, it's best to open either a 401(k) account or a traditional IRA plan.

Step 2 – Choose the right brokerage firm.

Always check the account fees, and choose the one with a great reputation and minimal fees. It's also best to choose a brokerage firm with great customer service.

Step 3 – Open your account.

You need to fill out some paperwork when opening your Roth IRA account. You'll need your social security number, driver's license, your bank's routing number, your employer's name and address, and the information of your beneficiaries.

Step 4 – Set up a monthly contribution system.

The next step is to deposit money into your Roth IRA. You can set up a monthly contribution schedule if your bank allows it. That way, you don't have to worry about depositing money into your investment account each month.

Take note that as of 2019, you're not allowed to contribute more than $6000 a year if you have an annual income of $189,000 or below.

Step 5 – Design Your Own Portfolio

Choose which stocks or ETFs you want to invest in. You can do this on your own, or you can consult a professional financial adviser who can help you make wise investment choices.

Traditional IRA vs ROTH IRA	
Traditional IRA	**ROTH IRA**
Tax-deferred	Tax-free
This means that it's not taxed now, but it will be taxed later when you decide to pull out your funds.	It's taxed now, but you'll be refunded for all the tax payments you've made when you decide to withdraw the funds.

This investment plan is for people who are in high tax bracket now, but will most likely be in a lower income bracket during retirement.	This investment plan is best for those who may be placed in a higher income bracket during retirement.
You must be under 70.5 years old to contribute	You can contribute at any age
Minors and non-working spouses can contribute	Non-working spouses and minors can also contribute

Annual contribution deadline: April 15	Annual contribution deadline: April 15

Simple IRA

SIMPLE IRA is the acronym for Savings Incentive Match Plan for Employees Individual Retirement Account. It is a tax-deferred investment account that allows you to save for retirement.

This employee-sponsored retirement savings and investment plan is usually offered by small businesses with 100 employees or less. Most small businesses favor SIMPLE IRA over the 401(k) plan because it is less complicated and a lot cheaper.

As previously mentioned, SIMPLE IRA is a matching investment program just like the 401(k) plan, but the matching and saving percentage is significantly lower than the 401(k) plan. Employees can only save up to 3% of their salary, and employers can contribute 2% of the employee's salary.

Let's say that you earn $100,000 a year. You can only deposit up to $3,000 a year and your employer has to deposit $2000 into your SIMPLE IRA account.

SIMPLE IRA has a contribution limit of $13,000 as of 2019. If you are over 50, you can add a catch-up contribution of $3,000.

Investing in a SIMPLE IRA is quite easy. You just have to check if your employer offers it and then sign up.

SEP IRA

A SEP IRA, or Simplified Employee Pension Individual Retirement Arrangement, is a retirement account used in the United States. This retirement plan is for small business owners and self-employed people. This retirement plan is mainly for entrepreneurs with one or two employees. But, it's also for freelancers and online sellers.

One of the best things about SEP IRA is that it has a higher contribution limit. As of 2019, you can save up to twenty 5% of your income or a total of $56,000, whichever is higher.

Spousal IRA

A spousal IRA is basically a traditional, or ROTH, IRA, but, this investment account allows a working spouse to deposit money on his/her working spouse's account.

To illustrate this point, let's look at Leslie and Josh's story. They are both nurses and met in the workplace. They fell in love and eventually got married. But, after a year, Leslie got laid off. To make sure that his wife has enough money for retirement, Josh decided to contribute money to Leslie's IRA.

This IRA type is perfect for stay-at-home spouses/parents, but you should take note that the Spousal IRA is not a joint account. So, even if Josh deposits money into his wife's IRA, the account is not his. This means that only Leslie could withdraw it.

Pros and Cons of IRA

One of the best things about IRA is that it has tax advantages. It's also easy to start and inexpensive. You can set up an IRA on your own without help from a financial planner.

But, the biggest disadvantage of IRA is that it has a contribution limit and low contribution rate. This means that you can only save so much through the IRA. It also has early withdrawal fees.

Taxable Brokerage Account

If you're serious about growing your wealth, you must have a taxable brokerage account on top of your tax-advantaged IRA and 401(k) plan.

A taxable brokerage account (or simply, brokerage account) is an investment account that you have to open through a brokerage firm. You can simply deposit cash into this account through checks or electronic fund transfers.

When you have a brokerage account, your broker will execute the trade orders (to either buy or sell stocks) on your behalf. Brokerage firms usually require a minimum account balance of about $500 to $2000. The money deposited into your brokerage account is called the money market fund. This amount just sits in your account until you decide to use it to buy stocks, bonds, and other securities.

A tax brokerage account can hold different types of investment products, such as common stocks, preferred stocks, bonds, real estate investment trusts (or REITs), exchange-traded funds (or ETFs), mutual funds, or certificates of deposit. We will discuss this in detail later in this book.

There are three types of taxable brokerage accounts:

A. Cash Account

This is the most basic brokerage account. When you have a cash account, you must pay all your investment transactions in full by the settlement date. This is perfect for beginners.

B. Margin Account

A margin brokerage account allows you to borrow money from the broker. The brokerage firm lends you capital that you can use to purchase stocks and bonds. This account allows you to invest more money in the stock market.

This brokerage account is riskier, and it's best for more experienced investors. Margin accounts also have a lot of requirements.

C. Option Account

This is a margin account that's used to buy and sell options or contract to buy. This account can be used for options trading at the Chicago Board Options Exchange. Investing through a taxable brokerage account has a lot of advantages, including:

- You can invest no matter what your income is.
- You can deposit (or contribute) as much as you want.
- You have a wide array of investment choices. This means that you can personally handpick the stocks and ETFs that you want to invest in.
- You can withdraw your money anytime without being liable for early withdrawal penalties. You don't have to wait until you're sixty.

To open a brokerage account, you just have to follow these steps:

Step 1 – Choose the brokerage firm you want to do business with.

Before you open an account with a brokerage firm, you must extensive research. You have to compare the incentives and costs. Check how much the brokerage firms charge per transaction. Choose a broker that charges minimal fees. This will save you a lot of money in the long run.

It's also important to look into the brokerage firm's services. Does the firm give you easy access to research data? Does the company support foreign training? Does it have an advanced trading platform that can be accessed through a mobile app?

Step 2 – File the paperwork.

After you've chosen the brokerage firm, it's time to fill out the new account application. You'd need your driver's license and your social security number. You also need to specify other information, such as your employment status, net worth, investment goals, and more.

Step 3 – Put funds into your account.

You can deposit money into your taxable brokerage account through an electronic funds transfer (or EFT), a check, or a wire transfer. You can also roll over your 401(k) plan into your brokerage account.

Step 4 – Choose the stocks and other securities you want to invest in.

Once you've already set up your brokerage account, it's time to choose the stocks you want to invest in and build your portfolio.

Pros and Cons of Investing in a Taxable Brokerage Account

One of the best things about investing in a taxable brokerage account is the fact that there's no limit to the amount of money that you can put in it. In addition, it does not have early withdrawal fees. The downside is that it does not have tax advantages. This means that there are no tax discounts and other privileges.

It's best to use a taxable brokerage account when you've maxed out your IRA or 401(k) plan. It's also perfect for those who want to retire early.

Direct Stock Purchase Plan

A direct stock purchase plan is an investment program that allows you to buy stocks directly from a company without a broker. This means that you don't have to deal with middlemen. Let's say that you want to purchase Company N stocks. Instead of opening a brokerage account, you just have to buy the stocks directly from the issuing company.

This plan is usually inexpensive and perfect for first-time investors. You'll only need around $100 to $500 to get started.

However, one of the worst things about the direct stock purchase plan is that it's not liquid. This means that you can't sell your stocks without using a broker, so this investment plan works best for long-term investors.

Here's how you can invest through a direct purchase plan:

Step 1 - Decide what stock you want to invest in.

Step 2 - Check the company's website, and go to the FAQ page to see if the company sells its stock directly. If yes, there's usually a link to the company's stock transfer facilitator.

Step 3 – Click on the link. This link usually contains the prices and the minimum amount of money required to open a direct stock purchase plan.

Step 4 – Create an account following the instructions on the company's website. You'll need your SSN, driver's license, name, and bank information.

Step 5 – Specify how many stocks you want to purchase and transfer money into your direct purchase plan.

Dividend Reinvestment Plan

A dividend reinvestment plan or DRIP is an investment program that allows you to reap the benefits of compounding. Investing in DRIP allows you to reinvest the dividends earned from your investments, resulting in more returns and investment profits. When you invest in a DRIP, your investment will grow exponentially.

Let's say that you invest in a few McDonald's stocks. McDonald's usually pays quarterly dividends to its investors. Now, if you sign up for DRIP, your quarterly dividend earnings are automatically used to purchase more Mcdonald's shares.

One of the best things about DRIP is that it increases your investment exponentially, so it won't sit idly. Plus, it has extremely minimal fees, if any at all. You don't have to worry about those hefty transaction fees that add up.

Chapter 2 Summary

Below are some summary points from Chapter 2.

To get started in stock market investment, you need to follow these steps:

- **Step 1** – Understand the difference between stocks and stock mutual funds.
- **Step 2** – Determine what your investing style is.
- **Step 3** – Set your investment budget.
- **Step 4** – Choose a brokerage firm and open an investment account.
- **Step 5** - Deposit money into your account and start investing.

There are many types of investment accounts that you can invest in, including a 401(k) plan, an IRA or individual retirement account, a tax brokerage account, a direct purchase plan, and a dividend reinvestment plan.

- The 401(k) plan is an employer-sponsored investment account. It has tax benefits. It comes with a matching program that allows employers to match their employee's contributions. This investment plan is inexpensive and hassle-free. You can simply sign up through your employer.

- The individual retirement account (or IRA) is a savings and investment account that comes with tax benefits. There are different types of IRA, such as the traditional IRA, the SIMPLE IRA, the Roth IRA, the spousal IRA, the self-directed IRA, the SEP-IRA, and the non-deductible IRA.

- The traditional IRA is a tax-deferred retirement investment account. This is something that you can open through a brokerage firm. You can use your traditional IRA fund to invest in mutual funds, stocks, and other securities.

- The Roth IRA is a tax-advantaged account. It is more flexible than the traditional IRA and offers more investment choices. You have to pay upfront taxes for your contributions, but you'll get a tax refund when you retire.

- The SIMPLE IRA is an investment account. It's also the acronym for Savings Incentive Match Plan for Employees Individual Retirement. It works a lot like the 401(k) plan in the sense that it also has a matching program. But, it's cheaper. Most small businesses offer this type of retirement plan.

- You should invest in a 401(k) plan if you're going to be in a lower tax bracket when you retire.

- The SEP-IRA (or simplified employee pension) is an investment plan for small business owners, self-employed individuals, and freelancers.

- The spousal IRA is just a regular traditional or Roth IRA. The difference is that it allows a working spouse to contribute to his/her non-working spouse's account.

- The direct stock purchase plan allows you to purchase stocks directly from issuing companies. This saves you a lot of money because you don't have to go through a broker.

- The dividend reinvestment plan, or DRIP, allows you to reinvest your dividend earnings. So, if you want your earnings to just keep on growing, you should choose this plan.

- The taxable brokerage plan is best for serious investors and high-income earners. But, if you're on a budget, it's best to go with employer-sponsored retirement savings and investment plans.

In the next chapter, we will discuss the basic stock investment strategies and how you can use them to grow your wealth.

Inspiration #3

"There are two types of people who will tell you that you cannot make a difference in this world: those who are afraid to try and those who are afraid you will succeed."
Ray Goforth

Please Kindly Review This Book

If you have found any value from reading this book, please kindly post a review letting us know about it. It'll only take a minute of your time. Thank you so much!

Chapter 3

Stock Investment Strategies

Stock market investing is one of the most powerful and effective ways to grow your money, but to achieve great wealth, you have to invest your money wisely. You must have a sound and foolproof investment strategy. Warren Buffet made a lot of money in the stock market because he is a wise investor. He has mastered the art of growing his money exponentially over time. Below are the top investing strategies that you can use to grow your money.

Value Investing

The best way to earn money from the stock market is to "buy low and sell high." This principle is at the heart of an investment strategy called value investing.

The principle behind "value investing" is quite simple. All you have to do is to find companies that are undervalued in the stock market.

To illustrate this point, let's say that Company V decides to go public. The stock market estimates its value at $100 million. But, having studied its earnings and products, you are convinced that it has an intrinsic value (investor's perceived value based on forecasted future earnings) of $1 billion. So, you decide to invest in Company V stocks.

Value investors believe that profit is best made by *investing* for the long haul (in high-quality companies), not by *day trading*. They take time to research and determine the value of company assets.

Value investors do not focus on external factors that can affect the company's value, such as daily price fluctuations and market volatility. They believe that focusing on high-value companies is the path to building great wealth.

Here are the key principles of value investing:

Value investors do not care about market speculation. They are not looking for the next best thing. They instead look for stocks that are undervalued, so they can earn huge profits in the future.

Stocks are mispriced all the time. For example, when some investors are scared, they blindly sell everything they own. This creates opportunities for savvy value investors to benefit from. Value investors look at the company's intrinsic value (the value of total assets) over its market value (stock price).

The key to value investing is research. You must know the value of the company's assets. You must also determine how the company is performing in comparison to its competitors and find the reason why the stock is sold at a discounted price.

Look for a company with a low P/E ratio, as it's *likely* to be undervalued. The P/E ratio is calculated as:

P/E Ratio = Market value per share/Earnings per share

Note: (/) represents the division sign.

It's best to invest in stocks with a P/E ratio of less than 40%. The stock's price should be no more than two-thirds (66.67%) of its intrinsic value.

Let's say that Company K has an intrinsic value of $1 million, and it has 10,000 shares. This means that its intrinsic value per share is $100, but its current stock price is currently valued at $50. Should you invest in company K? Yes, because its price is only 50% of its intrinsic value.

The company you invest in should have an annual earnings growth rate of 7%. Look at the company's earnings and make sure that its earnings are growing year after year.

It's hard to really determine the intrinsic value of a company. This is the reason why you should give yourself a margin of safety.

The margin of safety is calculated as:

Margin of safety = 1 – (Current stock price/Intrinsic stock price)

Let's say that Company H's current stock price is $40, but you think that its intrinsic stock price is $50. Your margin of safety is 20%.

The process of determining a company's stock value is based on a detailed and highly accurate analysis of the company's earnings and assets. Still, this process is lined with predictions and a little bit of speculation. So, you may come up with an inaccurate intrinsic value. This is the reason why value investors invest in companies with a high margin of safety. This minimizes the risk.

You should invest in a company with a low debt/equity ratio. The debt/equity ratio is a measure of the company's financial health. It is calculated by dividing the company's total debt by its shareholder equity.

Debt to Equity Ratio = Total Liabilities/Total Equity

If a company has a debt-to-equity ratio of $0.50, it means that it has a debt of $0.50 for every dollar of equity. Companies with a low debt to equity ratio are in good financial health because their *profits and earnings are significantly higher than their liabilities*.

Choose a company with a huge growth potential—one that hasn't tapped certain markets yet.

Be patient. Understand that time is your friend when it comes to value investing. This is why you have to be patient. You'll have to wait for months (if not years) to gain huge profits.

To become a successful value investor, you have to focus on the business, not on its stocks. This means that you should ignore stock trends and news.

You should stop analyzing the overall health of the stock market. You focus on the financial health and profitability of the company you want to invest in.

You must invest in companies that you believe in, love, and understand. And most of all, choose companies that are undervalued. This way, you'll earn huge capital appreciation profits in the future.

Pros and Cons

The major advantage of this investment strategy is that it creates a low-risk and high-reward scenario. Plus, it's less work in the sense that you don't have to be concerned about the day-to-day stock price fluctuation.

Value investing is a long-term investment strategy, so you get to pay a low tax rate on your investment earnings. You also get to save on transaction fees.

The downside of value investing is that it's sometimes difficult to identify undervalued companies. You have to do extensive research. It's also hard to come up with an accurate company valuation.

Growth Investing

Growth investing is an investment strategy that focuses on capital appreciation (or capital gains). Growth investors usually invest in emerging companies that have the potential to grow exponentially in the future.

Here are the top "growth investing" tips:

Tip 1 - Invest in innovative and fast-growing enterprises.
You should look for companies with revolutionary and ground-breaking technology. And you should invest during their early stages.

In 2012, a Facebook stock was valued at 26.62. At that time, Facebook was already big, but it's still growing. By, January 2019, it's valued at $165.71. So, if you bought 100 FB stocks for $2,662, you already have $16,571 in 2019. Not bad, right?

Tip 2 - Cut your losses as fast as you can.
You're going to make investment mistakes. Don't let your losses exceed 20%. If the price of the stock consistently drops day after day, get rid of it so you will not end up losing more and more money.

Tip 3 - Sell a winning stock when its price starts to go down.
When a stock reaches its peak, it will lose its momentum and its price will start to go down. Sell your stock right away when this happens. This will maximize your profit.

To illustrate this point, let's say that you bought 100 Company Y's stocks at $10 each. After one year, the stock price reached its peak at $80. At this point, you already have an investment profit of $7,000. That's not bad at all. So, if the price starts to go down, sell your stocks right before they decline by 20% (i.e., $64), your limit. This way, you can earn an optimal profit. If you wait for a few months, your profit could go down further.

Tip 4 - Long-term investments make more money.
Growth investors can make money in just a few months by investing in fast-growing companies, but you must be patient if you want to maximize your investment earnings.

Tip 5 - Diversify your portfolio.
Don't put all your eggs in one basket. You have to spread your wealth and invest in different companies in various industries. You can buy a few tech stocks, a few healthcare stocks, and you can invest in real estate properties. Diversifying helps to minimize your exposure to any industry/sector/investment vehicle.

Tip 6 - Buy more shares of your most profitable stocks.
You'll eventually build a huge portfolio over time. To maximize your profit, sell your low-performing stocks and buy more stocks of the best-performing companies in your portfolio.

Tip 7 - Invest in companies with a good profit margin.

Profit margin is calculated as:
PM = (Revenue − Expenses)/Revenue

You should invest in companies with a high-profit margin because these companies likely have a strong brand, are able to charge high prices for their products, and are keeping their costs low. You should avoid companies with a low-profit margin because these companies are not really earning much. They're just getting by.

Value investors invest in stable and established companies, while growth investors place their bets on companies with high growth potential. These companies are usually at their early stages, much like Facebook in 2012.

To be a successful growth investor, you should actively find unicorns—companies that produce innovative and revolutionary products and technologies.

Pros and Cons

One of the biggest advantages of growth investing strategy is that it's more likely to double your money faster.

Take Facebook as an example. In December 2012, an FB stock was valued at $26.62. A year later, its price had risen to $54. So, if you invested in an FB stock during its IPO, you've doubled your investment in just one year! Amazing, right?

But, investing in growing neophyte companies is risky. Plus, growth projection estimates are sometimes inaccurate and based on speculation.

Let's look at Theranos as an example. In 2003, nineteen-year-old Elizabeth Holmes dropped out of Stanford University to start a blood-testing company called Theranos. The company claimed to have developed a technology that could improve the efficiency, convenience, and affordability of blood testing and diagnoses.

It was a breakthrough, and Elizabeth Holmes became a celebrated Silicon Valley entrepreneur. She became the youngest female self-made billionaire. Theranos partnered with Walgreens and Safeway and built in-store clinics. Thousands of American people had their blood tested using the groundbreaking Theranos technology.

Theranos was a true *unicorn*. It was overvalued, but many growth investors believed that it was the future of blood testing and diagnostics, and so they invested in Theranos.

Theranos was a private company, but it had initially raised $6 million from investors. It raised a total of more than $600 million from investors. In 2014, the company was valued at $9 billion, making Elizabeth Holmes one of the wealthiest people in the world.

But there was something off about Theranos. First of all, Elizabeth Holmes was not a doctor or a medical professional. Second, the technology they used was vague. A whistleblower claimed that the capabilities of the company's supposedly groundbreaking technology were extremely exaggerated.

In 2018, SEC charged Elizabeth Holmes with fraud, and the company's investors lost more than $600 million.

Growth investing is a great strategy, but you have to be careful in choosing companies to invest in, as a lot of startup entrepreneurs exaggerate the capabilities of their technologies to lure investors.

Dividend Investing

Lydia is a Chinese-American living in New Jersey. Her husband, Peter, used to own a huge hardware and home improvement store in the city.

Lydia was living the American dream, living in a four-bedroom house in a great neighborhood. She was driving a nice car, and she could buy all the things she couldn't afford when she was in China.

Instead of splurging on designer bags, she decided to invest $500,000 in stable companies that paid annual dividends. After six months, Peter died in an accident. His business started to crumble after his death. Lydia was forced to close it.

It's a good thing that Lydia invested in companies that pay dividends each year. She has about $70,000 dividend earnings per year—enough to cover her mortgage payments and daily needs.

Dividend investing is an investment strategy that involves buying shares of companies that pay dividends. This strategy is best for people who just want to sit back and live off their passive income.

Here are the main principles behind dividend investing:

Invest in quality companies.

Don't invest in cheap low-quality stocks but high-quality ones. To get the most out of your money, you have to invest in companies that are in top financial shape.

You have to invest in a company with a low debt/equity ratio. You don't want to place your bet on a company that has no proven history of consistently paying dividends. You would want to invest in a company that raises its dividend payments year after year.

Invest in stable companies.

Remember that slow and steady wins the race. Don't invest in rising superstars. Instead, *invest in companies that have already weathered recessions and various economic setbacks*. Why? So you can sleep at night. Investing in steady companies decreases risk and gives you peace of mind.

Choose a company with a rising dividend yield.

As previously mentioned, a dividend yield is calculated as:

DY = Annual Dividend/Stock Price

So, if Company Z stock costs $100 and its annual dividend is $10, its dividend yield is 10%. To get the most out of your money, it's best to invest in a company with a high dividend yield.

Also, it's best to choose a company that has a dividend yield of at least 3%. This helps you keep up with inflation.

Better safe than sorry.

You have to pick a stock that has a high margin of safety because this minimizes your risk of losing money when slightly off with your valuation. Buy stocks at a price below their value. Avoid buying overpriced stocks to lower the risk.

Dividends are not everything.

As a general rule, you should invest in companies that pay a good amount of annual dividends, but you should not base your investment decisions solely on dividends. Remember that a big dividend payout is not always an indication that the company is a good investment. Why? Well, companies that are paying a huge amount of dividends are not reinvesting their revenues. This means that there's a low opportunity for growth. In addition, the company could be paying an unsustainable amount of dividends to cover up for poor financial performance (because greedy and unsuspecting investors won't care to investigate)

Aside from the dividend payments, you should also consider the company's growth potential and financial health. You should invest in companies with rising revenue and a low debt/equity ratio.

You should remember that at the end of the day, dividend stocks are just like other stocks. They are volatile, and they are susceptible to the ups and downs of the stock market.

Pros and Cons

The biggest advantage of dividend investing is that it can provide a steady and reliable income stream. You'll most likely get a check once or twice a year. Seeing a huge amount of money deposited into your bank account every quarter is exciting and exhilarating.

But, keep in mind that companies can cut dividend payments any time if they're experiencing a setback or decrease in revenue. Dividend payments are not guaranteed, so you must not rely on dividend payments alone. Dividend payments are taxable, so taxes can eat away at your returns.

Also, the prices of dividend stocks, such as Coca-Cola, Colgate-Palmolive, Johnson & Johnson, and AT&T are quite stable. This means that there's not much opportunity for growth or capital appreciation.

Sure, it's great to get a quarterly dividend payment of 3%. But, when you're investing in dividend stocks, you may be giving up the opportunity to earn higher returns from capital appreciation.

Let's look at Lauren and Kelly's story to illustrate this point. In 1997, Kelly bought 100 Coca-Cola stocks at $28.94 each. She invested a total of $2,894. She was sure of her investment, as Coca-Cola was one of the most stable companies in the world and paid dividends, too.

Kelly's friend, Lauren, decided to invest in a relatively new online bookstore called Amazon. She invested in 1000 Amazon stocks at $2.34 each. Her total investment was $2,340.

In 2019, both Kelly and Lauren decided to sell their shares. Kelly earned dividends along the way and sold her stocks at $48.38. She had a total capital appreciation profit of only $1944 in 22 years.

Lauren, on the other hand, sold her 1000 Amazon stocks at $1,638.88 each. She has a total capital appreciation profit of $1,635,660. Amazing, right?

This story reminds us that dividend payment is good. But, when you invest in dividend-paying companies, you could miss out on opportunities to earn huge capital appreciation profits.

For a more detailed treatment of Dividend Investing, see the book – <u>Dividend Investing For Beginners: Learn The Basics Of Dividend Investing And Strategies In 5 Days And Learn It Well</u>

Day Trading

Day trading is an investment strategy that involves buying and selling stocks and other securities on the same day. There was a time when the only people who could do this were those working for brokerage firms and huge financial institutions. But, with the advent of the internet, pretty much anyone with internet access can participate in day trading.

As we discussed earlier in this book, the price of a stock is determined by the law of supply and demand. Each time the stock is traded, its price changes.

A stock has a daily opening and closing price. The opening price is the price upon which a stock first trades when the stock market opens on a trading day. The closing price, on the other hand, is the price of a stock when the stock closes on a trading day. The balance between a stock's supply and demand fluctuates several times within a day. This is the reason why a stock's price can either go up or go down in just a few minutes.

Let's say that Company Z's stock price is pegged at $10 on December 10, 2018, at 9:30 A.M. when the NYSE opens that day, but, due to rising demand, its stock price rises to $15 at 4:00 P.M. just before the stock market closes.

If you bought 100 Company Z stocks at 9:00 A.M. and decided to sell them at 4:00 P.M., you'd earn a capital appreciation profit of $500. Not bad for a day's work, right?

Benefits of Day Trading

It allows you to learn.

Day trading is a great opportunity to test a wide variety of trading techniques and patterns. It helps you learn from your mistakes quickly.

It helps you avoid overnight risk.

The stock price can fluctuate from five to 10% overnight. And remember, a lot of things can happen in just one night. A scandal can happen. Political issues can arise. Day trading eliminates these risks and helps you sleep like a baby at night.

It's a great home-based business.

As previously mentioned, you can do day trading online, so it can be a great home-based business.

It gives you psychological satisfaction.

You'll feel an adrenaline rush when you start earning a significant amount of money in just a few hours. It gives you a kick and a sense of accomplishment. Day trading is exciting, and it's good for your ego.

It's relatively easy.

You don't need to have a PhD in finance to do day trading. Plus, you don't have to be a licensed trader if you're trading penny stocks (stocks that trade under $5). If you're good with stock charts and recognizing patterns, then you have a good chance of doing well.

You can see results faster.

You don't have to wait for months or years to see the fruits of your investment. You can earn profits in just one day.

You become your own boss.

Day traders usually work alone, and they own their time. They have a flexible working schedule, and they work at their own pace. Day trading is great for people who want to become their own boss.

Day trading is also a high-risk investment strategy. You can earn a lot of money in just one day, but you can lose a lot of money too.

Day Trading Success tips

Do your homework.

Remember that knowledge is power, especially in day trading. You must do extensive research before you place your bet on a stock. You must also study market volatility and trends.
List all the stocks you want to trade, and track these companies. Check business news often. It's important to keep yourself informed.

Determine how much risk you can tolerate.

You must decide how much you're willing to risk on each transaction or trade. Many seasoned day traders risk only about 1% or less of their account per transaction.

Let's say that you have a $50,000 investment account and you're willing to risk 0.5% of your account. This means that your maximum loss per trade should be $250 ($50,000 x 0.005). Do not risk more than $250.

You must set aside a lot of time.

You have to watch the prices go up and down by the minute. This is the reason why day trading requires a lot of your time. This is not something that you can do on the side. So, if you have a full-time job, this investment strategy is definitely not for you.

You have to start small.

It's best to start small. You have to focus on just one or two stocks during your first few transactions. Don't trade three or more stocks in one trading day.

You can also invest in fractional shares to minimize your losses. For example, if an Apple stock costs $60, you can buy ½ of the stock for $30 instead of purchasing one full stock.

Be realistic.

Don't expect to earn ten thousand dollars per day. You can't win all the time. In fact, a lot of traders only win 60% of their trades. You just have to make sure that your wins are bigger than your losses.

Don't let the stock market get on your nerves.

Day trading is sometimes stressful and frustrating. Stay cool. Do not let your fears and greed get the better of you. Also, don't be too optimistic or hopeful. You should use logic in making investment decisions, not emotions.

Pros and Cons

Day trading is exciting. It gives you an adrenaline rush. It also helps you earn money in just a few hours. It's easy to get into, and you can do it in the comfort of your home.

That said, day trading is a bit tricky because of market volatility. You can earn a lot of money in just a few hours, but you can also lose a lot of money. A lot of day traders incur financial losses in the first few months. This is the reason why you have to do extensive research before you start trading.

Day trading is often costly. To achieve great success in day trading, you have to invest in a high-quality trading platform and software. You also have to pay a commission fee for every trade.

Day trading sometimes gives you a natural high, but it's also stressful. You'll have to use multiple computer screens so you won't miss trading opportunities.

Short Selling

Short selling (also called going short) is an investing strategy that involves the sale of a stock that the investor has borrowed. It is a strategy that helps investors profit from a stock's decline. It's the complete opposite of the "buy low, sell high" investing principle.

When you invest in a stock, you're placing your bets on the company. When you short sell, you're betting against the company. You short sell because you expect the price of the stock to go down.

To illustrate this point, let's look at Nathan's story. Nathan was doing extensive stock research and heard a rumor that Company X was in deep financial trouble. After some research, he had good reason to believe the company's stock price would go down soon, so he decides to short sell Company X stock to profit from his stock price prediction.

Nathan called his broker, John, and told him that he wanted to short ten Company X shares. John needed to find ten Company X stocks to lend to Nathan.

To find stocks for Nathan, John looked at his client's portfolio and his stock inventory. John found ten stocks in one of his client's investment portfolios. He then sold the share in the market for Nathan at its current market price of $150 each. The $1500 revenue from the sale was credited to Nathan's brokerage account.

As it turns out, Nathan was right. After seven days, Company X's financial struggles were made public and its stock price dropped to $75.

After the stock price dropped, Nathan wants to make a profit from his prediction by buying back the stocks he sold through his broker. Nathan calls John and tells him to cover his position in Company X. John then uses the money in Nathan's brokerage account to buy ten Company X shares at the current price of $75 each. He then returns the borrowed stocks to his client's portfolio.

Nathan sold ten Company X stocks for $1500 and bought it back for $750. So, he made a profit of $750, minus a small fee paid to John for all the trouble. That's awesome, right?

Pros and Cons

Short selling is a great investment strategy for pessimists and skeptics. One of the best things about short selling is that it allows you to earn a huge amount of money without an upfront cost. And most of all, it allows you to make money out of failing companies.

However, you should know that short-selling is a risky investment strategy. You won't know for sure if your prediction is correct. You'd end up losing money if the value of the stock you short sold were to rise dramatically. Also, short selling (and the pessimism that comes with it) can lead to a stock market crash.

You don't have to use just one investment strategy. You can mix up different investing strategies to get maximum returns. You can also test each strategy to find out which one works best for you.

Chapter 3 Summary

To grow your wealth, you have to use an investment strategy that works for you. You can also mix and match different strategies. There are many investment strategies that you can use, including dividend investing, day trading, value investing, short-selling, and growth investing.

Value investing is one of the best investing strategies. It's used by seasoned investors like Warren Buffet. Its main principle is "buy low, sell high." Value investors actively look for undervalued stocks. They also invest in stable and established companies. They do not look at market trends, and they do not worry about stock price volatility. They do not care about stock market predictions.

Value investing is a great way to minimize risk, but it can cause you to lose the opportunity to earn huge capital appreciation profits from rising "superstar" companies.

Growth investing is the opposite of value investing. Growth investors place their bets on companies that are growing quickly. They are constantly searching for "unicorns" or the "next best thing" in business. To minimize risk, you have to sell a winning stock once it starts to go down. You must also build a diversified portfolio consisting of companies that are performing well in the stock market.

Growth investing gives you an opportunity to earn a lot of money, but it's risky, too.

Dividend investing is an investment strategy that involves investing in companies that pay dividends annually or quarterly. It's also important to choose a company with rising dividend payments.

Day trading is an investment strategy that involves buying and selling stocks on the same day. This strategy helps you profit from market volatility. It also gives you the opportunity to learn and sharpen your trading skills. The downside of this strategy is that it's time-consuming and you'll have to invest in an advanced trading platform.

Short-selling is an investment strategy where an investor profits from falling stock prices. The investor borrows stock from his broker and sells it at the current market price. Once the stock price goes down, he buys back the stock and returns the stock he borrowed. His profit is the difference between his selling price and buying price.

Short-selling is great because you don't have to pay for anything upfront. But, it's too risky. You won't know exactly if the stock goes down anytime soon. If the stock price does not go down, you'll end up with more debt than you can handle.

To lower the risk, you have to invest in companies with a low debt/equity ratio and a high margin of safety. These companies are financially healthy.

To maximize your earnings, it's best to diversify your investment portfolio and mix and match different strategies.

In the next chapter, you'll learn how to pick the right stocks.

Chapter 4

How to Choose the Right Stocks to Invest In

Mia worked in a software development company for fifteen years. She's good at her job, but she was always stressed and tired. So, she decided to give stock market investment a try in order to build a passive income portfolio that would help her retire early. She met with an old friend named Kate, a financial analyst. Kate helped her invest in high-quality and fast-growing stocks.

After two years, Mia had earned $650,000 capital appreciation profit. She quit her job and traveled around the world. She soon used part of her earnings to establish her own graphic design company. Her $650,000 grew to over $2 million.

Mia is living her dream life. She owns her time. She has a successful business, and she even bought a beach house in Miami.

Chloe was Mia's former colleague. Like Mia, she's been working in the software development industry for about fifteen years. She was also tired. After she heard about Mia's success, she decided to invest in stocks, too.

Chloe didn't know anything about the stock market and didn't know how to choose the right stocks. She invested in companies that were buried in debt and engaged in unethical business practices. So, she ended up losing $10,000.

A lot of people get rich through stock market investment, but many people lose huge amounts of money too. This is the reason why you should be careful in choosing the right stocks to invest in. You have to be clear about your investment goals and use the right strategies that work for you and match your risk tolerance level. You must also do extensive research before you place your bet on a stock.

Setting an Investment Objective

Before you start investing, you should be clear about what your investment objectives are. You should also decide what type of investor you want to be. Do you want to be a long-term investor? Or, do you want to be a day trader, trading stocks by the minute?

You must be clear about what you want to achieve through stock market investing. How much are you willing to invest? How much do you want to earn each year? What are you willing to risk?

You need to set financial goals like how much you want to earn in one year or in five years. You should also set non-financial goals. Why? Well, your investment earnings are just mere tools that you can use to support your non-financial goals. So, what do you want to achieve? Do you want to have a grand wedding? Do you want to travel to a foreign country at least twice a year?

Factors to Consider in Choosing a Stock

The key to building a profitable investment portfolio is choosing the right stocks. When you're starting, buying individual stocks is costlier than investing in low-cost mutual funds. Below are the factors that you should consider in choosing stocks to invest in.

Growth in Earnings

Before you invest in a company, you should check its earnings and make sure that it's consistently growing over time. The growth doesn't have to be huge. You just have to look for an upward trend in earnings.

For example, let's say that you have an extra $3,000 and you want to invest it in stock. You're looking to invest in two companies. Company A is one of the biggest steel manufacturers in the country, while Company B produces the nation's best-selling batteries.

Take time to examine the data below:

Company A: Leading Steel Manufacturer	
Year	Earnings
2005	$2,158,111,202
2006	$2,160,369,000
2007	$2,080,250,000
2008	$1,988,910,000
2009	$1,888,630,121
2010	$1,780,980,011
2011	$1,761,918,870
2012	$1,709,919,450
2013	$1,670,980,689
2014	$1,659,658,905

2015	$1,640,050,814
2016	$1,590,010,110
2017	$1,550,000,289
2018	$1,499,110,980

Company B: Leading Battery Manufacturer

Year	Earnings
2005	$750,000,905
2006	$805,963,960
2007	$815,750,690
2008	$909,530,066
2009	$915,784,210
2010	$918,974,560
2011	$990,741,632
2012	$1,101,890,390
2013	$1,156,120,450
2014	$1,190,110,000
2015	$1,220,000,980
2016	$1,240,780,360
2017	$1,310,000.550
2018	$1,399,222,080

If you look closely, you'll see that Company A has a lot more earnings than Company B. However, its revenue has been declining since 2008. This means that the company is facing problems. It could be mismanagement or a decreasing market share due to an aggressive competitor entering the space.

Company B, on the other hand, has had steady growing earnings since 2006. This company is doing something right and is more worthy of your hard-earned money.

Stability

Sir Tim Berners-Lee published a paper about a proposed information management program called the "internet" in 1989. He then implemented the first successful communication between a Hypertext Transfer Protocol (HTTP) and a server a few months later.

In 1990, Berners-Lee began writing the World Wide Web (www)—the first-ever web browser. The next year, he launched the first-ever web page. This forever changed the world. This is what stock market players call a black swan.

According to risk analyst Nassim Nicholas Taleb, a black swan is an event that's hard to predict that can forever change the world. And if you're wise enough to predict or at least spot a black swan at its early stage, you're going to win big in the stock market and in business. This explains why early internet entrepreneurs like Jack Ma and Jeff Bezos are extremely wealthy.

And soon, promising internet companies decided to go public and the investors went crazy placing their eggs in the "internet business basket".

But after the tech industry got a little too crowded and the world experienced a stock market crash in 2008, the revenues of internet companies became volatile. So, a lot of investors ended up losing huge amounts of money.

Even so, this is just an example. It doesn't mean that you shouldn't invest in the tech industry. All companies are bound to lose their stock value at some point, especially during periods of recession and economic crisis.

To achieve long-term success in the stock market, you have to invest in companies that are strong and stable enough to endure unfavorable economic conditions. Erratic stock price fluctuation is not a good sign.

To illustrate this point, look at the graph below:

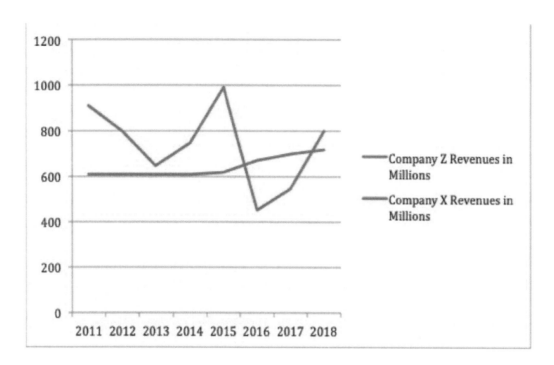

Notice that Company Z's revenue doesn't fluctuate as much as Company X's. This means that it's more stable and a good choice for long-term investment.

The Company's Market Share

Before you invest in a company, look at its market share. Is it one of the strongest in its industry? Is it doing well against its competitors?

If you want a big return on your investment, it's best to invest in strong market leaders, such as Microsoft (software), JPMorgan Chase (finance), Facebook (communication), Las Vegas Sands (casino and resorts), Gilead Science (biotech), PepsiCo (beverages), Comcast (cable and broadcasting), and Marriot (hotels).

Profitability

You should not only look at a company's total earnings but its profits. Are the earnings higher than the costs? How much profit does the company make per sale? Does the company have a positive cash flow (the amount of money going in is greater than the amount of money going out)?
You should also examine the company's profitability over the years. You would want to invest in a company with an upward profit trend.

Price to Earnings Ratio or P/E Ratio

P/E Ratio is the stock's price divided by its earnings. For example, if a company's stock costs $50 and each investor gets paid a yearly dividend of $5 per stock, its P/E Ratio is ten (fifty divided by five).

P/E ratio is usually used to measure a company's growth potential. If the P/E ratio is high, it means that investors are willing to pay huge amounts of money for each stock. This could increase the stock price in the future and result in a high return on investment (ROI).

Companies with a low P/E ratio have minimal growth potential. This means that you could possibly lose money when you invest in them.

However, do take note that not all companies with a high P/E ratio have promising growth potential. These companies may just be overvalued.

The P/E ratio is a great tool that can help you decide which stock to invest in, but you should not rely on it entirely.

The Company's Leadership

Like it or not, the company's leadership can greatly affect its future. This is the reason why you should also look into the competency of the company's management team.

Do you feel that the company leaders are competitive and competent? Do you think the company is well managed? Is the company ahead of its competitors because of innovation? Do you see the company leaders as visionaries?

You should also look at the company's culture. Does the company have a toxic environment? Is it involved in scandals and lawsuits?

Debt to Equity Ratio

As previously mentioned, equity is the difference between the company's assets and its liability.

Let's say that Company Y's asset amount to $100,000, but the company's liability amounts to $80,000. This means that the company's equity is valued at $20,000.

The debt to equity ratio is used to measure a company's leverage and overall financial health. To calculate it, you need to divide the company's total liabilities by its equity.

Assets	Liabilities	Equity
$100,000	$80,000	$20,000

Now, look at Company B's data above. If you divide the company's liabilities by its equity, you'll find that its debt to equity ratio is $4. This means that Company B has a $4 debt for every $1 of equity. Therefore, Company B is not in good financial health and not fit for long-term investment. It's too risky.

To minimize risk, you should invest in a company with a debt-equity ratio of 0.30 or below.

Dividend Payments

As previously mentioned, not all companies pay dividends, but those that do are usually more stable and in good financial health.

It's good to invest in companies that pay dividends, but, you have to be careful. High dividend yields could indicate instability. It can also mean that the company is stagnant, as it's not reinvesting its profits on growth and expansion.

Company Reputation

Avoid companies who engage in unethical practices. Companies with a bad reputation are most likely to get involved in scandals.

Company Executives' Investing Habits

Look at the number of shares that the executives and CEOs are buying or selling to know what's really happening inside the company. If the CEO is selling his shares, it could mean that the company is in deep trouble.

Positive EPS

As previously mentioned, earnings per share, or EPS, is the portion of profit allotted to each common share. A positive EPS is an indicator of a corporation's profitability.

It is usually calculated as:

Earnings per share = Net Income/Number of shares

But, the more accurate calculation is:

Earnings per share = (Net Income - Preferred Dividends)/ Weighted Average of Outstanding Common Shares

The weighted average of common shares is more accurate because the number of shares changes over time. The company can create new shares in the middle of the year. This data is usually found in the company's income statement, balance sheet, or financial statement.

Look at the data below:

Company D				
Assets	Liabilities	Net Income	Preferred Dividend Payments	Weighted Average Outstanding Shares
$200,000	$35,000	$165,000	$20,000	10,000 stocks

So, if you calculate Company D's EPS, it should be like this:

$$\text{EPS} = (165,000 - 20,000)/10,000$$
$$= \$14.5$$

Company D's EPS is actually a good number, considering that stock market giant Apple has an EPS of $6.45.

You can use the first formula to simplify things. This formula is not as accurate as the second one, but it gives you a pretty good number that you can use to track the profitability of a potential investment opportunity.

Tips to Picking the Right Stocks

Remember that when you buy a company's stock, you become a part-owner of that company. So, you have to look at the overall health of the company you want to invest in. Below are a few tips that you can use in picking the right stocks:

Invest in what you know.

You know why you're choosing a particular clothing brand over the other. You also know the ingredients of the dishes you order from your favorite restaurant. To avoid losses, it's important to invest in a stock that you know well.

Before you invest in a stock, you need to answer the following questions:
- Do you know what products the company offers?
- Have you examined the company's financial statements?
- Is the company profitable?
- Is it buried in debt?
- Do you trust the company executives?
- Is the company innovative?
- Would you buy its products?

Avoid overhyped companies.

You already know what happened to Theranos. Like Theranos, Dropbox is also one of the most celebrated Silicon Valley unicorns. Its stock price was at $30 on May 31, 2018, but it dropped to $19.96 on January 1, 2019. Hyped companies can be great, but the truth is, not all of them can live up to the hype.

Consider the price.

Seasoned investors often look for stocks that are undervalued. As a general rule, stocks with a P/E Ratio of fifteen and below are considered cheap, while stocks with a P/E of more than twenty are considered a bit overpriced or expensive.

But you should remember that cheap is not always good and expensive is not always bad. Sometimes, stocks are cheap simply because they're not performing well, and some stocks are expensive mainly because they're growing fast. Think Amazon. As of February 2019, an Amazon stock trades at $1,500. Yes, it's expensive, but it's worth every penny as it is the world's most valuable public company.

Evaluate the financial health of the company you're investing in.

You must start looking into the company's financial reports. Keep in mind that all public companies release quarterly and annual financial reports. You can easily access these reports through the SEC website. You can click on the link below:

https://www.sec.gov/edgar/searchedgar/companysearch.html

Pick a company with a huge profit margin.

The profit margin is the difference between the company's revenue and expenses. You would want to invest in a company that manages its expenses well.

Do not forget to sell your stocks.

Profit is the ultimate goal of stock market investment, but you should be clear about how much profit you want to make.

Let's say that you bought Company G's stock at $10 and you want to earn a $5 profit. So, when the stock price hits $15, you have to sell right away. Don't be greedy or you'll end up losing a lot of money in the future.

You should believe in the company's management.

Don't invest in a stock if you don't trust the company's CEO. It's really just that simple. Use logic, but also listen to your intuition. Don't invest in anything that doesn't feel right.

How to Tell When a Stock is Overvalued

A lot of financial analysts often overestimate a company's value. You can lose a lot of money if you invest in overpriced stocks.

But how do you know if a stock is overvalued? Well, you have to review the company's annual financial report, income statement, and balance sheet.

The first thing you want to look at is the stock's P/E Ratio (also called the earnings multiple). Overvalued companies usually have a higher P/E. If a company's stock price is twenty times its earnings, it's definitely overvalued.

To illustrate this point, let's look at two companies—Company M and Company N.

Company M's stock price is $150 while its earnings per share are $200. Therefore, its P/E ratio is 0.75. It's too low, as its "earnings per share" are actually bigger than its price.

Company N's stock price, on the other hand, is pegged at $200, but its earnings per share is only $10. It has a PE ratio of twenty. This means that its price is twenty times its earnings.

If you're a growth investor, you'll most likely go for Company N because it has high growth potential in terms of the stock price. It means that investors are optimistic and are willing to pay a high price for its stock.

But, if you're a value investor, you'll most likely invest in Company M because it's undervalued.

A lot of investors just look at the P/E ratio to determine if a company is overvalued, but there are also other ways to check if a company is priced way above its intrinsic value.

Look at the company's PEG ratio. The Price/Earnings to Growth ratio, or PEG ratio, is calculated as:

PEG Ratio = PE Ratio/EPS Growth Rate

This metric is used to evaluate a company's stock price compared to the company's growth and earnings. The lower a company's PEG ratio is, the better.

Let's say that Company W has a P/E ratio of twenty. That's quite high, right? But it has an EPS growth rate of 25%, so its PEG ratio is 0.80. This means that its price is cheap relative to its potential growth.

This metric is best for investors who consider both the company's value and growth rate.

Check the company's dividend-adjusted PEG ratio.

If you're investing in a company that pays dividends, you have to look at its dividend-adjusted PEG ratio. It is calculated as:

Dividend-Adjusted PEG Ratio = PE Ratio/(Earnings per Share Growth Rate + Dividend Yield)

Let's say that Company J has a P/E ratio of twenty, and it has an "earnings per share" growth rate of 10%. It has a dividend yield of 2%. So, its dividend-adjusted PEG ratio is 1.66. It's pretty low. It means that its price is relatively low relative to its dividend yield and growth rate.

Examine the relative dividend yield.

As previously mentioned, the dividend yield is computed as the annual dividend per share divided by its current stock price.

For example, if Company Z's stock price is $10 and it pays $1 per share each year, its dividend yield is 10%.

The dividend yield serves as a signal. You see, highly profitable companies often pay higher dividends. This is the reason why stock market beginners can use the dividend yield to examine the company's price relative to its profits.

So, if a company has a high dividend yield, it's most likely undervalued. If a company has a low dividend yield, it's overvalued.

Let's say that you own 100 shares of Company D stocks with a dividend yield of 5%. To maximize your profit, you have to carefully track the company's dividend yield. This helps you determine the profitability of the company. If the dividend yield drops to 2% or below, it means that the business is not earning well, it's overvalued, and it's best to let that stock go.

Check if the company is part of a cyclical industry.

Some industries are extremely sensitive to the ups and downs of the economy. These industries are called cyclical industries because their profits go up when the economy is good and it goes down during an economic crisis.

Companies in cyclical industries usually have unique characteristics. They thrive when the economy is good. Automobile companies, construction contractors, and steel factories are examples of cyclical industries.

When the economy is good, companies in cyclical industries appear to have fast-growing profits and a low P/E ratio. So, it would seem that the company is undervalued, but this situation is actually a "value trap" and can be dangerous and tricky. While this can easily deceive stock market beginners, more experienced investors know that the P/E ratio of these companies is much higher than they appear.

So, before you judge a company based on its P/E ratio, you must first determine if that company is in a cyclical industry. If so, don't take all the data you see at face value.

Check the company's earnings yield.

Earnings yield is calculated as earnings per share divided by the current stock price.

Earnings yield = Earnings per Share/ Current Stock Price

If you look at the formula carefully, you will notice that it's the reverse of the P/E ratio. This metric helps investors determine the return on an investment. You can also use this to check if a stock is overvalued.

You can compare a stock's earnings yield with the ten-year treasury yield. If the earnings yield is less than the treasury yield, it's overvalued, but if a company's earnings yield is high, it's undervalued relative to bonds.

Many investors use earnings yield to make investment decisions. This metric helps you determine if it's best to invest in stocks or you should go with other securities, such as bonds.

Buying an overvalued stock is incredibly risky. You could end up losing a lot of money. So, before you place a bet on a stock, make sure that it's reasonably priced and not overvalued.

How to Build a Stock Position

A stock position is the number of stocks owned by a dealer, an organization, or an individual. When you buy a stock, you are basically taking on a position. There are two types of positions—long positions and short positions.

As we discussed earlier, the term "going short" refers to a process where you *borrow* a stock and sell it, hoping that the price will go down. When you're "going long", you're basically purchasing the stock (and paying for it upfront) because you're hoping that its value will go up.

So, a short position is done when a stock is borrowed and then sold. A long position, on the other hand, is done when a stock is owned and then sold.

There are many strategies that you can use to build a winning or extremely profitable position. One of the ways to do so is through "pyramiding." You see, if you gulp an entire cup of hot coffee, you'll burn your mouth. So, you have to take small sips to avoid getting burned. You can use this same strategy to minimize your losses and maximize your return, and it's called pyramiding.

If you find a high-performing stock, don't invest all your money in it right away. You have to test the water to avoid losing all your money.

Let's say that you found a good stock and you decided to invest $5,000 to buy 100 shares at $50 each. If the stock price falls 10%, you'll lose $500, but if you invest just ¼ of your investment money, you'll only lose $125.

Pyramiding involves making multiple stock purchases to build your position. The best way to do this is by dividing your purchases into three to five installments.

Let's say that you have a $10,000 investment fund. When you enter a trade, you can use $3,000 to purchase stocks and build your initial position. Make sure to use this money to buy stocks of market leaders and established companies.

Now, don't buy more shares until the price of your current position moves up to at least 2%. Once this happens, invest another $3000. At this point, you have already invested 60% of your investment fund.

Once you earn another 2% capital appreciation profit, invest another $2,000. And invest the last $2,000 after the stock price has increased by another 2%.

This investment strategy is smart. It maximizes your returns, reduces risks, and limits your losses. Pyramiding is an investment strategy to build a winning stock position.

Another way to build your stock position is to write (sell) put options.

A put option is an option to sell stocks at an agreed price on or before a particular date. So, when you're writing a put option, you're essentially obliging yourself to buy shares at a specific price.

To explain this, let's say that you want to buy a few Company V shares. You did extensive research and you found out that the best way to earn maximum profits from your investment is to pay no more than $20. But, there's just one problem: Company V stock is currently valued at $50.

If you're a beginner, you'll most likely wait until the price drops to your desired price. But, if you're an advanced investor, you won't just sit around and wait until the stock price goes down. You can write put options for Company V shares at $20. When you do this, you're essentially promising another party (it could be a bank, a corporation, a mutual fund, or an individual investor) to buy his Company V shares when it reaches $20.

But, why will you do this? Well, in exchange for your commitment, the buyer of your put option contract will pay you a premium per share. One put option contract usually covers 100 stocks. So, if you write five put options (total of 500 stocks) and the buyer pays you a premium of $2 per stock, you'll earn $1,000 (500 stocks x $2). You'll also just have to pay a minimum commission fee.

Writing put options is a great way to build your stock position because you'll always be a winner no matter what the outcome is.

If the put option expires and never gets exercised, you get to keep the $1,000.

If the stock price declines temporarily and the put option contract is executed, you get to purchase the stock you like at a heavily discounted price. Instead of paying $50 for it, you'll just pay $20 minus the $2 premium. So, you'll pay $18 and get $32 ($50-$18) discount per stock. Not bad, right?

If the company decides to close before the stock price reaches $20, you'll still keep the $1000.

Writing put options is a great way to win in the stock trading game.

Chapter 4 Summary

To win big in the stock market, you have to invest in the right stocks. Otherwise, you'll end up losing a lot of money.

Set an investment objective. What do you want to achieve? You have to set financial goals like how much you want to earn in a year or in five years. You must also set non-financial goals like how often you want to travel or the experiences you want to be able to afford.

When you're choosing stocks, you have to consider different factors such as growth in earnings, stability, the company's market share, profitability, the P/E ratio, insider activity, the company's reputation, and the trustworthiness of the company executives.

To pick the right stocks, you have to invest in what you know and avoid over-hyped companies. These companies are usually overvalued and can't live up to the hype. You should also consider the stock price and the profit margin.

You need to sell your stocks once the price reaches its peak. This technique maximizes your profit.

Avoid overvalued stocks. Look at the PEG and the P/E ratios to determine if a company is overvalued.
- If a company has a high P/E ratio, it's overvalued.
- A company with a high PEG ratio is also overvalued.

You must also determine whether or not the company is in a cyclical industry. Companies in a cyclical industry are highly sensitive to economic cycles. Its price is high when the economy is good, and it decreases when there's a recession.

When the economy is great, cyclical stocks appear to have fast-growing revenues. This decreases its P/E ratio, giving you the impression that the stock is undervalued when, in reality, it's overvalued. When you're looking at the P/E ratio of companies in cyclical companies, don't regard it at face value. It can be deceiving.

If a stock's earnings yield is lower than the Treasury Yield (bond), it's overvalued.

Avoid buying overvalued stocks. It's also wise to sell overvalued stocks in your portfolio.

A stock position is the amount of stock an investor owns. There are two types of positions—long and short.

A long position involves buying a stock and paying for it upfront. A short position, on the other hand, involves borrowing stocks and selling them in anticipation of a price decline. Once the price drops, you buy stocks to cover what you borrowed. The difference between your selling price and buying price is your profit.

Writing put options is one great way to build your stock position. A put option is the right to sell a stock at a specific price. So, if you want to buy stock A for $20, but its current price is $30, you can write a put option and sell it. The buyer then has the right to sell you his stock when the price goes down to $20 before the expiration date of the contract. The buyer pays you a premium fee for your promise. If the price doesn't go down and the contract is never executed, you can still keep your premium earnings. So, there's nothing much to lose.

In the next chapter, we'll talk about brokerage account and statement in detail.

Inspiration #5

"Success is walking from failure to failure with no loss of enthusiasm."
Winston S. Churchill

Chapter 5

Understanding Your Brokerage Account and Statement

You'd be surprised to know that most extremely wealthy people have taxable brokerage accounts. It provides an avenue for them to benefit from the stock market and diversify their income stream. As we've discussed earlier in this book, if you want to invest huge amounts of money and be a successful investor, you have to open a taxable brokerage account.

What is a Brokerage Account?

A brokerage account is a taxable investment account that you can use to buy and sell stocks and other securities. As the name suggests, it's opened through a brokerage firm. It's much like a bank account. You have to deposit money into your account before you can start buying and selling stocks.

You can deposit money into your account through checks or electronic funds transfers. You can also wire money to your account.

Type of Investments a Brokerage Account Can Hold

Brokerage accounts are not just for stocks. There are a number of securities that a brokerage account can hold, including:

Common stock – This represents partial ownership of a company. It usually comes with voting rights.

Preferred stock – This stock usually comes with high dividend payments, but it's more expensive than a common stock. Preferred stock shareholders typically don't have any voting rights.

Bonds – A bond is a debt security. When you purchase a bond, the issuer (usually a government entity) owes you money. You earn money from bonds through interest rates.

Mutual fund – A mutual fund is funded by different shareholders. It's basically a pool of money that's invested in different securities. It's relatively easy to invest in a mutual fund. Plus, it's usually managed by a financial professional. You can buy different mutual funds, too, so you don't have to put all your money into one mutual fund.

ETF – An ETF, or Exchange Traded Fund, is a basket of different securities that's traded as a stock. An ETF is a good investment because it has trading flexibility. It helps you diversify your investment portfolio and manage risk. It's also cheaper than a traditional mutual fund.

REIT – A real estate investment trust, or REIT, is a company that either finances or operates income-producing real estate properties, such as commercial buildings. REITs usually own various income-generating real estate companies, such as hospitals, warehouses, hotels, and malls. You can invest in publicly traded REITs using your brokerage account.

Money market and certificate of deposit – A money market account generally represents pools of liquid mutual funds. It has higher interest rates and has a limited check-writing capacity. A certificate of deposit is basically a time deposit. For example, you agree to deposit $10,000 into your account. You can't withdraw that amount for five years, but, you'll earn an interest rate throughout this period. So, if you earn $1,000 in interest per year, you're going to earn an extra $5,000 for your deposit after five years.

Cash Brokerage Accounts and Margin Brokerage Accounts

There are two main brokerage account types—cash accounts and margin accounts. A cash brokerage account requires you to deposit cash into your account. You'll have to pay for your transactions in cash and in full when you have a cash brokerage account.

A margin account, on the other hand, allows you to borrow from the broker using some of your assets as collateral to buy securities.

If you're a beginner, it's best to go for a cash brokerage account. Why? Well, margin brokerage accounts are complex and will get you buried in debt if you're not careful.

Limits of Money You Can Deposit in a Brokerage Account

As previously mentioned, other investment plans such as the IRA and 401(k) have limits, but taxable brokerage accounts do not, so you can deposit and invest as much as you want. That said, keep in mind that you do have to pay taxes for this type of investment.

How Many Brokerage Accounts Can One Have?

You can have as many brokerage accounts as you want, but, keep in mind that most brokerage firms require a minimum deposit amount of $500 to $2000, so opening multiple accounts can be costly.

However, if you have unlimited resources, you can open multiple accounts with different brokerage firms.

Difference between a Discount Broker and a Full-Service Broker

There are two general types of broker:
- A full-service broker and
- A discount broker.

A full-service brokerage account is great because it comes with a dedicated broker. You can call, text, or email him should you want to make an order. This broker usually knows you personally, and sometimes he knows your family. He also knows your finances intimately. He's like a financial advisor. You usually have to meet him regularly to discuss your portfolio.

Full-service brokers usually charge high commission fees. A discount broker, on the other hand, doesn't charge much. But, this type of broker usually operates online. A discount brokerage account is like a Do It Yourself (DIY) investment plan.

So, what should you choose? Well, it depends on what your priority is. If you are on a budget and you really want to save money, it's best to open a discount brokerage account. But, if you really want to have a financial adviser, it's a great idea to open a full-service brokerage account.

Understanding Your Broker's Statement

A broker's statement is a monthly report that contains the activities in your brokerage account. You can choose to receive a paper statement, but you can usually just check it online as well.

It pays to examine your statement carefully so you can spot some kind of fraud. When you first receive your income statement, you have to check to see if it looks professional. An unprofessional-looking statement is a red flag. Legitimate brokerage firms invest time and effort to make sure that their reports look polished and professional.

Here's what you'll find in your broker statement:

- **Statement period date** – A broker's statement reports how your investment is doing at a specific period of time, usually a month. If you don't see a statement period date, that's a red flag.

- **Account number, account name, and address** – This obviously contains your taxable brokerage account number, your name, and your present address. Be worried if this information is incorrect.

- **Contact information** – This contains the contact information of your broker. If you don't see this anywhere in the statement, the brokerage firm you're dealing with may be dubious.

- **Name of the clearing firm** – This contains the name and the contact number of the clearing firm that holds your investments. FINRA rules require brokerage firms to place this information in their statements. So, be alarmed if you don't see this anywhere in your statement.

- **Account summary** – This provides insight with regards to how your account is doing. This can help you review and assess your investment decisions.

- **Fees** – This covers the transaction and commission fees you've paid within the time period.

- **Account activity** – This is where you can see the stocks you've bought or sold within that particular time period.

- **Margin** – If you have a margin account, you'll find this section. This contains the amount you've borrowed to purchase stocks and other securities.

Portfolio detail – This section breaks down your investment by type like stocks, bonds, or mutual funds.

Chapter 5 Summary

A brokerage account, as the name suggests, is an investment account that you open through a brokerage firm. You can use this account to buy and sell stocks in the stock market.

A brokerage account can hold different types of securities, such as common stocks, preferred stocks, bonds, mutual funds, REITs, ETFs, and certificates of deposit.

There are two main types of brokerage account—cash and margin. You need to pay for everything in real-time if you have a cash account. A margin account, on the other hand, allows you to borrow money from a broker.

There are two general types of brokers—discount and full-service. Discount brokers simply interact with you online. Full-service brokers, on the other hand, conduct face-to-face meetings on a regular basis.

If you want to save a lot of money, it's best to open a discount brokerage account. But, if you need guidance in choosing the right stocks, it's a good idea to choose a full-service brokerage firm.

You have to examine your broker's statement carefully to spot fraudulent activities or inconsistencies.

In the next chapter, you'll learn how to read your broker trade confirmations.

Inspiration #6

"The trick is not to learn to trust your gut feelings, but rather to discipline yourself to ignore them. Stand by your stocks as long as the fundamental story of the company hasn't changed."
Peter Lynch

Chapter 6

How to Read Your Broker Trade Confirmations

The SEC requires all brokerage firms to provide their clients broker trade confirmations. But what are these, and why are they so important to understand?

What is a Brokerage Trade Confirmation?

Once you start trading through your broker, you will receive a trade confirmation, which will generally be mailed to you. If you opted for the paperless option, it will be sent to you in the form of a PDF document. This document will be delivered to you each time your broker buys or sells a stock on your behalf.

Here are the things that you can find in your trade confirmation:

- The name of the stock you've traded along with its ticker symbol. (A ticker symbol is an abbreviation used to identify a stock. For example, Facebook's ticker symbol is FB while Amazon appears as AMZN in NASDAQ.)
- The total stocks you have either bought or sold in that transaction
- The price per share
- Commission paid to your broker
- The date of the transaction
- The total gross value of the transaction. (How much did you pay for or earn during this transaction?)
- The net value of the transaction. (How much did you pay or earn after the commission fees?)
- Your account number
- The type of order you used. Did you do a market order or a limit order?

You must look at your trade confirmations carefully. This way, you'll know if your broker executed the orders according to your instructions. Contact your broker right away if you think that there's some kind of mistake.

Your trade confirmations can be useful when you file your taxes. This is the reason why you should always keep the original copy of your trade confirmations.

Chapter 6 Summary

Every time you want to buy or sell a stock, you'll receive a trade confirmation in the mail.

Your trade confirmation usually includes information regarding the name of the stock and its ticker symbol, the price per share, the total number of stocks traded, commission payments, account details, the net value of the transaction, and the type of order made.

You have to examine that carefully to make sure that your broker executed your order flawlessly.

You must also keep copies of your trade confirmations because you'll need them when you file your taxes.

In the next chapter, we will discuss the different types of trades that you can place with your broker.

Inspiration #7

"Go for a business that any idiot can run—because sooner or later any idiot probably is going to be running it."
Peter Lynch

Other Investing Books By Michael Ezeanaka	
Book #	**Book Title**
1	Dividend Investing For Beginners – Learn The Basics Of Dividend Investing And Strategies In 5 Days And Learn It Well
2	Real Estate Investing For Beginners – Earn Passive Income With REITS, Tax Lien Certificates, Lease, Residential And Commercial Real Estate
Download The Audio Versions Along With The Complementary PDF Document For FREE from www.MichaelEzeanaka.com	

Chapter 7

Types of Trades You Can Place with Your Broker

Once you have deposited money from your brokerage account, you're now ready to buy and sell stocks. To do that, you have to place an order with your broker. There are many types of orders, such as market orders, limit orders, stop orders, stop-limit orders, day orders, and trailing stop orders. Let us review each one of them.

Market Orders

A market order is a request to purchase or sell a stock at its current market price. It is the most standard stock order, and it has to be executed right away.

For example, when you place a market order to buy 100 Company H stocks at the current price, your broker has to execute the order right away. As long as there is someone willing to sell Company H stocks, your buy order will be executed right away.

Let's say that you own fifty Company M stocks, and its price is dropping slowly, so you decide to sell it. You then place a sell market order. Your order will be executed right away—as long as there's someone willing to buy Company M stocks.

One thing that you have to remember when you're placing a market order is that you cannot control how much you pay for a stock. Several factors and stock market players determine the stock market price.

Limit Orders

A limit order is an order to either buy or sell a security at a specific price during a specific time period.

Let's say that you own 100 Company C stocks that are currently valued at $100. At this time, your position is valued at $10,000. To maximize your profit, you decide upon a limit order to sell fifty stocks when the stock price increases to $185. Then, you place another limit order to sell the rest of your shares when the stock price increases to $220. If the stocks reach your desired stock price, you'll earn a total profit of $10,250 from the investment.

If the stock price were to reach $185 but didn't make it to $220, you'd still earn a profit of $4250 and get to keep fifty Company C stocks.

Now, let's say that you want to buy 100 Company X stocks. Its current price is $100 each. You did extensive research and found out that the only way to maximize your investment profit is to purchase the stocks at $50 each. So, you place a buy limit order at $50. So, your broker buys the stocks for you once it hits $50 or below. If the stock price doesn't drop to $50 on a specific date, your order expires and doesn't get executed.

One of the best things about a limit order is that it maximizes your profit and also controls your losses. It's also a great technique to use if you want to "buy low and sell high."

All-or-None Orders

An AON is an order that has to be carried out entirely or not executed at all.

Let's say that you want to buy 1000 Company W stocks, but, only 500 stocks are available in the market. Your AON order doesn't get executed unless there are 1000 stocks available in the stock exchange. This order is active until it's either executed or canceled.

Stop Orders

Stop orders are also known as "stop-loss orders." It is an order to sell or buy a stock once it reaches a specific price (also called the "stop price"). It is designed to limit and manage your losses.

Let's say that Katya owns ten Company V stocks, which are currently valued at $50 each. Now, let's say that the stock price starts to go down and Katya is on vacation, exploring an exotic European island. Luckily, she did set a stop-loss order of $40. So, once the stock goes down to $40, the broker sells it.

Stop orders are different from the limit order. Limit orders are made to maximize profits, while stop orders are done to minimize losses.

Stop Limit Orders

A stop-limit order combines a limit order and a stop-limit order. To do this, you have to enter two prices—a limit price and a stop price. When the market reaches the stop price, your order becomes a limit order.

For example, Company G's stock is currently valued at $50 and trending up. You want to take advantage of this trend and, at the same, time try to maximize your profits. So, you place a stop order with your broker and ask him to start buying Company G stocks when they reach $55 apiece but stop buying when the price reaches $57.

In this example, the stop price was set at $55 and the limit price was set at $57. When you place a stop-limit order, the "stop price" initiates an action (either to buy or sell a stock) and the "limit price" stops the order.

A stop-limit order is designed to help limit your losses.

Selling Short and "Buy to Cover Orders"

As previously discussed in this book, selling short is the act of selling a borrowed stock in anticipation of a stock price decrease. Once the stock price decreases, a "buy to cover" is made to cover and return the borrowed stock.

Let's say that an investor called Caleb heard that Company H was engaging in bad business practices and that it was going to get exposed soon. This secret was kept from the public, so the company's stocks were still doing great in the stock market. In fact, one Company H stock cost $200.

So, Caleb called his broker and placed a short trade for ten Company H stock. His broker took ten stocks from his stock reserve and sold them for $200 each. He then placed the $2000 revenue in Caleb's brokerage account.

After a week, Company H's evil ways were made public and its stock price decreased to $40. Caleb then placed a "buy to cover" order for ten stocks. The broker bought ten stocks for $40 each (using money in Caleb's brokerage account). He then returned those shares to his portfolio. For this transaction, Caleb earned $1600 profit (minus a nominal sum paid to his broker for the trouble).

One of the biggest advantages of this strategy is that it doesn't come with upfront costs.

Day Order

A day order, as the name suggests, is an order to either buy or sell stock any time during the trading day. This order automatically expires if it's not executed within the day.

So, let's say that you placed a day order to buy a Company W stock when the price dropped to $10, but it never reached that price, so the order automatically expired when the stock exchange closed at 4:00 P.M.

Extended After-Hours Trading

A stock exchange usually opens at 9:00 A.M. and closes at 4:30 P.M., but there's such a thing as "after-hours" trading. It's completed after the stock exchange closes, and it's usually done via ECN or Electronic Communication Network. You can still trade via ECN from 4:15 P.M. to 8:00 P.M. You can also trade through ECN 100 minutes before the stock exchange opens from 8:00 am to 9:15 am.

Extended after-hours trading helps you take advantage of market volatility or some news that happened after stock market hours.

For example, Jared owns 100 Company G stocks valued at $100 each, but at 4:00 P.M., he saw breaking news that the company CEO was charged with fraud. He immediately logged into his account and placed a market order to sell his 100 stocks at the current market price. Good thing he did because the next day at 9:00 A.M., the stock price has already dropped to $50. Jared would have lost half of his money.

GTC Order

GTC means **good 'till canceled**. A GTC order is active until it's manually canceled by the investor. Let's say that you want to buy a Company R stock at $20, but its current price is $80. So, you place a GTC limit order to buy a stock if its price is to drop to $20. This order is going to be active (even after a few years) unless you cancel it.

Trailing Stop Orders

A trailing stop order is a complicated animal, but don't worry. I'll explain this the easiest way I can.

The trailing stop order is the more advanced form of the "stop order" and has a "trailing amount."

A sell stop order has a stop price below its current market price with a specific trailing amount. Sounds complicated, right? Well, to illustrate this point, let's say that Carly owns one Company S stock valued at $400 when she bought it. Her sell stop price is set at $800.

When the stock finally reaches $800, Carly is already ready to sell her share, but Company S is really doing well, and she doesn't want to miss the opportunity of earning more profits. So, she places a $40 trailing stop. This follows the stock price upwards. But, if the stock drops by $40, the broker then sells Carly's stock. Let's say that after the stock reached the limit of $800, the stock price kept rising. After a few days, it reached $1,200. But three days after, it dropped to $1,160. So, this is the cue for Carly's agent to sell the stock.

The table below will help you understand this concept:

Carly's Stock S Portfolio		
Date	**Stock Price**	**Action**
Aug 1	$400	Carly purchased the stock and placed a sell limit order at $800 with a trailing amount of $40
Aug 2	$450	
Aug 17	$800	Reached the stop limit
Aug 18	$950	
Aug 19	$1200	
Aug 20	$1190	
Aug 21	$1180	
Aug 22	$1160	The stock price dropped $40 from its peak price of $1,200 so the broker sells

		the stock to maximize Carly's profits

Bracketed Orders

Bracket orders are designed to lock in your profit and limit your loss by bracketing the orders. It's basically three orders bundled into one. This order allows you to enter into a position with a target and stop loss.

Remember that bracketed orders are limit orders, so you have to set a limit price, a stop price, and a target price. You can also set a trailing stop loss amount.

The best thing about this order is that it helps reduce your risk and minimize your losses.

How to Place and Cancel an Order

To place an order, you just need to fill out an order form. You have to specify the amount of the order and the order type. You must also set limit or stop prices if you're doing a stop or limit order.

To cancel the order, you just have to log in to your account. Go to your order. There should be an option to cancel the order. Click on that, and you're good to go.

Chapter 7 Summary

There are different trades that you can place with your broker, such as limit order, market order, stop order, stop-limit order, and trailing stop order.

A market order is the most basic order. It has to be executed immediately at the current market price.

A limit order is an order to either sell or buy a stock at a certain price during a certain time period.

An AON order, or all-or-none order, has to be carried out entirely or not at all. Hence, the name.

A stop order helps you manage your loss. It is an order to either buy or sell a stock once it reaches a certain price called the "stop price." It's similar to a limit order but different in the sense that stop orders minimize losses while limit orders maximize profits.

A buy-to-cover order is an order that's typically used in short selling. It's an order to buy stocks to cover the ones that were borrowed during a short sale.

A day order expires at the end of the trading day.

The stock exchange closes at 4:00 P.M, but you can still trade via the electronic communication network, or ECN, during extended trading hours—4:15 P.M. to 8:00 P.M. and 8:00 A.M. to 9:15 A.M.

GTC stands for good 'till canceled. This order remains active until the investor cancels it.

A trailing stop order helps you specify the amount of profit you're willing to let go.

A bracketed order bundles three orders.

You need to fill out a form to make an order.

To cancel an order, you need to log in to your account, go to the order, and click on cancel. This process varies depending on what type of brokerage account you're using.

In the next chapter, we'll discuss the research process and how you can use macroeconomic and microeconomic analysis to make wise investment directions.

Inspiration #8

"Look for small companies that are already profitable and have proven that their concept can be replicated. Be suspicious of companies with growth rates of 50 to 100% a year."
Peter Lynch

Chapter 8

How to Research Stocks to Purchase

You can't go to war without a weapon. You can't just buy a stock; you must do extensive research. You must learn to be your own stock analyst. This will help you make wise and sound investment decisions.

To do comprehensive stock research, you must apply two methods used in economics—micro-economics analysis and macro-economic analysis.

Macro-Economic Analysis

As discussed earlier in this book, economic forces (such as the law of supply and demand) affect stock prices. So, before you invest in a stock, you have to use a top-down global research approach. You must look at the global trends. You must look at the big picture.

As of this writing, Airbnb is not a public company yet, but for the purpose of discussion, let's assume that it is. A lot of cities in Europe and in the United States have banned Airbnb, but it continues to grow in various cities in the world. In fact, you can find a lot of great Airbnb deals in Bali, Malaysia, Singapore, Zurich, Mykonos, and Faro. Plus, it still has a number of untapped markets. If you look at the big picture, you'll see that Airbnb is still a great investment because of its huge growth potential.

Aside from looking at the company's global overview, you must also consider other factors, such as:

Interest Rates

When the interest rate is high, it would be more costly for companies and individuals to pay their debts. This decreases their disposable income and their spending. This also affects business revenues and can drive down the stock prices.

But, when a country has a low-interest rate, people have more disposable income. They'll end up buying more stuff. This could lead to an increase in stock prices.

However, you have to take note that rising interest rates can benefit specific industries, such as the financial sector—banks, mortgage companies, lending companies, and insurance companies.

The Cyclical Nature of an Industry

Before you buy a company's stock, you have to determine if that company belongs to a cyclical industry.

Cyclical sectors such as the automobile industry and the construction industry are sensitive to the ups and downs of the economy. When the economy is good, their prices go up, but they go down when there's a recession.

Try to avoid investing in companies in cyclical sectors (unless you're very good at timing your investments). You'd want to invest in a stock that can withstand economic setbacks.

Stock Market Index

As previously discussed, an index tracks the performance of market leaders. So, in essence, it reflects the overall health of the stock market. If an index is trending up, it means that stock market players are a bit optimistic and a bull market may be happening.

Industry-Wide Research

Let's say that you want to invest in luxury brands such as Louis Vuitton (LVMH) or YSL. Before you do that, you must look into the overall health of that industry.

If you look closely, you might discover that luxury brands are not doing as well as they used to be because of online shops and China-made products.

Micro- Economic Analysis

When you do macro-economic analysis, you are looking at the economy and the industry, but understand that micro-economic analysis uses a "bottom-up" approach. This means that you have to do extensive company research.

You have to look into the different aspects of the company, such as:

The Company's Product – Is the product good? Does it have loyal customers? Is the product going to be relevant ten years from now? Let's say that a music store is selling its stocks. Would you buy? Well, let's face it: no one buys CDs anymore. We just download music from the internet or check YouTube. Technology is changing by the minute. A widely used product may become irrelevant and unnecessary in the next few years. Just look at what happened to diskettes.

Sales and Revenue – Is the company earning money? Are their products doing well in the market?

Debt to Equity Ratio – Is the company's debt bigger than its equity? If so, then you should run as fast as you can.

P/E Ratio – If the company has a high P/E ratio, it means that it has high growth potential. However, it also means that the stock is overvalued. A low P/E ratio means that the company has low growth potential, but it also means that it's overvalued. If you're into growth investing, choose a company with a high P/E ratio. But you have to choose a company with a low P/E ratio if you're into value investing.

Earnings per Share (EPS) – A company with high EPS is really doing well. It's profitable. So, assuming other factors check out (e.g., it's not using a lot of unsustainable debt to generate the earnings), it's a good idea to invest in a company with a high EPS.

Company Management – Do you trust the people managing the company? Do they engage in unethical business practices? If you don't trust the people running the company, then avoid it at all costs.

Also, make sure that the company's profit has been trending upward at least in the last five years.

Chapter 8 Summary

You must do comprehensive research to determine if a stock is a good investment. To do this, you must use two methods—macroeconomic analysis and microeconomic analysis.

To do *this*, you must first look at the worldwide trends. Are the global trends favorable to the stock you're purchasing?

You must also look at the interest rates. Higher interest rates often drive stock prices down.

Don't invest in a company that belongs to a cyclical industry. Cyclical sectors are susceptible to changes in the economy.

Micro-economic analysis involves extensive company research. You should look at the company's income statement. Is the business earning profits? You must also look at the company's products. Are they doing well in the market?

In the next chapter, we will discuss the signs that a stock is a good investment.

Inspiration #9

"The most important quality for an investor is temperament, not intellect. You need a temperament that neither derives great pleasure from being with the crowd or against the crowd."
Warren Buffett

Please Kindly Review This Book

If you have found any value from reading this book, please kindly post a review letting us know about it. It'll only take a minute of your time. Thank you so much!

Chapter 9

Signs a Stock is a Good Long-Term Investment

You'd be surprised to know that most extremely wealthy people have taxable brokerage accounts. As we discussed earlier in this book, if you want to invest huge amounts of money and be a successful investor, you have to open a taxable brokerage account.

A company is profitable when its revenue is higher than its expenses and debts. To illustrate this point, let's look at Miranda's story. She was passionate about fashion, and so she decided to build her own bag company.

Miranda started her company with only $70,000. This covered pretty much all of her expenses. She operated her business online, so she didn't have a lot of fixed costs. She didn't borrow anything from the bank. In her first year, her company earned $150,000. This means that she had a profit of $80,000 (revenue minus expenses).

Now, let's look at Mark's story. He had a tour bus company operating in Patagonia, Argentina. In one year, he spent a total of $10 million, half of which was borrowed from the bank.

Unfortunately, there were fewer tourists that year and he only earned $8 million. This means that his expenses were higher than his revenue, and he wasn't earning any profit.

Now, if you were an investor, which business would you invest in? If you looked at the revenue alone, you'd see that Mark's revenue was way higher than Miranda's, but Miranda was earning profit. Mark, on the other hand, was operating at a loss. In addition, the tourist industry can be a bit cyclical, as tourism seems to peak during the summer/festive periods whereas bad sales can show consistent sales all through the year. All other things being equal, a wise investor would choose to invest in Miranda's company.

So, how do you know if a stock is a good investment? Well, you have to look for these signs:

High returns on capital with little or no leverage

Leverage is a technical term for borrowed capital. When you're looking for a company to invest in, you have to choose a company that generates high returns on capital with minimal leverage.

This means that you have to choose a profitable company with extremely low debt. You do not want to invest in a company that's buried in debt—especially unsustainable ones.

Competitive advantage

Let's say that you are looking to invest in the organic food delivery service industry. You believe that it's the next best thing.

Company Z and Company A are both in the organic food delivery service business, but Company A's ingredients are sourced from a third-party farm while Company Z has its own farm.

In this scenario, Company Z has a competitive advantage because its production cost is lower and its ingredients are fresher.

To win big in the stock market, you have to choose a company whose products have a competitive advantage. It could be that their products are cheaper, more advanced, or simply more delicious.

You should also invest in companies with high levels of brand loyalty. For example, a lot of customers prefer using an iPhone even if Huawei is also producing high-quality products. Let's look at eBay and Amazon. They are almost the same. They are both great. However, Amazon is more successful than eBay because it has created something called "customer obsession." It has created a shopping platform that keeps the customers obsessed and craving more.

Investing in a company with a huge following can lead to great wealth in the future.

The company keeps its shareholders satisfied

Sadly, a lot of companies keep their shareholders in the dark about what's really happening in the company. Just look at what happened to Theranos.

To avoid losing your money, you must invest in a company that puts the interest of its shareholders before the interest of employees, suppliers, and even customers.

You would want to invest in a company with a management team that has your best interest at heart. You don't want to invest in a company with executives who have no qualms about squandering the organization's assets and resources.

How can you tell if management is on the side of shareholders? One way to go about it is to look at the annual report for previous years. How correct were their estimations? what promises were made? Were the promises kept? How honest and transparent were they about ongoing issues? Etc.

The company has a strong balance sheet

The economy experiences a cycle of ups and downs every now and then. Sometimes, the economy is good. Sometimes, it's bad. To minimize risk and maximize your profits, you have to invest in a company that can withstand difficult economic conditions.

But, how do you determine a company's financial health? Well, you have to look at its balance sheet. You should invest in a company with high shareholder equity. This means that its earnings are far more than its debts.

Choose a company with high revenue, high equity, low expenses, and low debts. Companies with this type of profile tend to have a very strong balance sheet.

Look at the company's market capitalization

Market capitalization or market cap is the total dollar market value of all the company's outstanding shares. It is calculated as:

Market Cap = Company's Outstanding Shares x Current Market Price

A lot of new investors look at the stock price to measure the value of a company, but this is just a mistake. The stock price is simply not enough. To determine the true value of the company, you have to look at its market cap.

Let's look at IBM and Microsoft as an example. As of February 2019, IBM's stock price is at $136.99, while Microsoft's stock is pegged at $107.01. If you just look at the price, you'll think that IBM is more valuable. However, Microsoft has a market cap of around $800 billion while IBM has a market cap of more or less $130 billion. Market capitalization helps to paint a clearer picture with regards to valuation.

Aside from the market capitalization, you must also look at enterprise value (EV). EV is calculated as:

EV = Market Value + Preferred Stock Equity + Debt + Interest – Cash and Investments

This metric is usually used by investors who want to acquire a certain company. But, it's not enough to look at a company's market capitalization alone. You must also look at market cap and enterprise value in relation to its net income (revenue – debts and expenses). You would want the two numbers to be as reasonably close as possible. Why? Well, it's wise to invest in a reasonably valued company. You not only want to invest in a company that's huge in terms of market cap; you also want to make sure that this company is actually earning money and in great financial health.

Best Stocks for Long-Term Investment

Throughout this book, we've discussed the many things that you have to consider in choosing the right stock for long-term investment. Not only should you choose a stock with hefty market capitalization, but you should also choose a company that produces and sells strong and established brands. Why? Well, these companies usually have a competitive advantage and they're most likely to survive trying economic times.

A List of Potentially Great Companies for Long-Term Investment

Starbucks Corporation (SBUX)

In the United States, you'll probably see a Starbucks shop on every corner. So, one would think that it has reached its growth plateau, but that's not true at all. In fact, Starbucks has a lot of growth opportunities abroad—especially in Asia. Many hedge fund experts, including Bill Ackman, think that Starbucks is still one of the best stocks to invest in.

Nike (NKE)

We all know that Nike is one of the biggest shoe brands in the world. The brand is worth $29 billion. It is in perfect form. In fact, the company's revenue has increased from $16 billion to $24 billion in just five years.

But Nike has a market share of 19% in the retail footwear market. So, it's definitely great for long-term investment.

And, if you invested $2000 in Nike stocks ten years ago, you'll have around $12,310 today.

FedEx (FDX)

FedEx is one of the biggest courier delivery service companies in the world. The massive growth in online shopping has vastly increased the demand for this company's shipping services, and as a result, its stock share price has increased by over 65% from 2015 to 2018. This is definitely one to explore further.

Costco (COST)

As we all know, Costco is one of the most popular membership-based warehouse shopping clubs. You could buy just about anything at Costco—fashionable jewelry, fresh flowers, sofas, flat-screen TVs, watches, vacuum cleaners, and prescription drugs.

Costco has about 760 branches worldwide as of 2018, and it has over ninety-four million members. What's more? Costco's earnings have grown over the years with more growth excepted heading into 2020. The company has twenty new warehouses planned for 2019 and is also entering the Chinese market.

In addition, the company also sells low-value *essential* items, which should help reduce the negative impact on its earnings during periods of economic weakness.

Coca-Cola (NYSE: KO)

Coca-Cola was invented in 1886 by a pharmacist named John Pemberton, who died two years later. His partner, Frank Robinson, worked hard to market this invention, but it just wasn't successful.

After Pemberton's death, Asa Griggs Candler rescued the business, and believe it or not, Coca-Cola was once marketed as a drug and remedy for headache and fatigue.

But, today, the Coca-Cola Company is one of the biggest soda manufacturers in the world. It's not the number one soda in the United States, but it's doing really well overseas.

Procter & Gamble (NYSE: PG)

Procter & Gamble is one of the biggest companies in the world and carries a number of household brands, such as Head & Shoulders, Tide, Olay, Ariel Detergent Powder, Joy, Safeguard, Pampers, Downy, Pantene, and more.

Procter & Gamble has a dividend yield of 3%, and it has a low P/E ratio. This means that its stocks may be undervalued. This is a great opportunity to multiply your investment over time.

Netflix (NASDAQ: NFLX)

Remember when cable killed VHS? Well, Netflix is about to kill cable TV. This streaming service company has grown over the past ten years. Its market cap is now bigger than stock market giants like Disney and Comcast, but it still has a lot of room for growth.

General Motors Company (GM)

If you invested $2,000 in General Motors stocks in 2012, you would already have grown that sum to $4,400 as of November 2018. Many people think that General Motors' glory days are long gone. That's not entirely true.

GM caught a lot of flak late in 2018 when management announced a major restructuring of its North American operations. Five factories would be idled as GM shifted production away from lower-margin cars like Cruze and Impala, and toward higher-margin trucks and SUVs.

GM would take between $3 billion and $3.8 billion in up-front charges to make these changes. In exchange, though, the company hoped to grow its annual cash flow by as much as $6 billion by 2020, giving it more resources to invest in high-margin and breakthrough technologies in the future, and also more financial flexibility to weather any recession that may be impending.

This is why I think GM is great for long-term investment. Although the up-front costs may be big, and the political fallout from layoffs unpleasant, GM is making strategic moves that will drive better profitability, as well as improve cyclical resilience.

Lowe's Companies, Inc. (NYSE: LOW)

Lowe's Companies Inc. is the second-largest home improvement company in the world, serving more than $17 million customers in the United States and in Mexico.
Over the past few years, Lowe's has developed a wide array of products, such as tools, home-building materials, home maintenance products, paint, and décor.

Lowe's has a 2.2% dividend yield, and it has an approximate 21% five-year dividend growth rate, which makes it an attractive prospect to explore further.

Apple Inc. (NASDAQ: AAPL)

Apple is currently the third biggest smartphone producer in the world, next to Samsung and Huawei. But, it's clearly one of the most powerful tech companies in the United States. Apple has an approximate 33% dividend growth rate in three years and offers a 1.7% dividend yield.

Coupled with the fact Apple is one of the most innovative companies in the world and commands a strong balance sheet as well as brand loyalty, it's a very attractive stock for long-term investment.

Chapter 9 Summary

To choose the right stock to invest in, you must look at the company's profitability.

You must also pick a company that has high returns and low or no debt.

Choose a company whose products have a strong competitive advantage. You would want to invest in a company with high customer loyalty rates.

Pick a company that keeps shareholders satisfied.

You must also look at the company's balance sheet.

The next chapter talks about the most powerful portfolio management strategies that you can use to manage your investment portfolio.

Inspiration #10

"The secret to being successful from a trading perspective is to have an indefatigable and an undying and unquenchable thirst for information and knowledge."
Paul Tudor Jones

Chapter 10

Portfolio Management Strategies

You can't rely on luck. To win big in the stock market, you've got to have a strategy. You must use logic and do extensive research. Below are the most powerful portfolio management strategies that you can use to grow your money and make the most of your investment portfolio.

Strategy 1

Don't Use Your Emotions in Making Investment Decisions

Charlie is a seasoned stock market investor and has earned a lot of money in the past from his investments in the manufacturing industry.

After a few decades of winning in the stock market, he decided to invest in sports stocks. He studied different sports stocks, including Madison Square Garden Co. (MSG).

MSG owns five professional sports teams, including the New York Knicks. Its stock value is a bit volatile and changes frequently, so it's not great for long-term investment.

But Charlie is a die-hard New York Knicks fan, so he invested in MSG and eventually lost a lot of his hard-earned money.

You're going to lose a lot of investment opportunities if you let your emotions cloud your judgment. You must be extremely objective when you're deciding which stocks to invest in. You must set your personal preferences aside and look at the numbers.

You can support your sports team all you want, but don't buy a team's shaky stock just because you're a die-hard fan.

Strategy 2

Diversification

The wise men of Wall Street always say, "don't put all your eggs in one basket." Why? Well, if you lose that basket, you'll end up losing all your eggs.

You should spread your wealth. For example, if you have an investment budget of $20,000 don't spend it all on FB stocks. Buy different stocks and other securities. You can invest in a few stocks and a little bit in bonds and certificates of deposit.

One of the cheapest and easiest ways to diversify your investment is to invest in a mutual fund. You can also invest in exchange-traded funds, or ETFs, and real estate investment trusts, or REITs.

It's also wise to invest a little bit of your money in index funds. The best index funds like the S&P 500 allows you to own a little bit of the highest performing stocks.

You should also keep building your portfolio. Use your investment profits to expand your portfolio and buy more securities.

Strategy 3

Stop Losses

Lara owns 100 Company Y stocks that she bought at $600/share. After a few months, the stock price rose to $800. This earned Lara a profit of $2,000 ($8000 - $6000).

Lara felt that she could already relax, so she went on a two-week Caribbean cruise. She did not check her account while still on a holiday. When she came back from her vacation, she learned that Company Y's stock price dropped to $400. She ended up losing a total of $2,000.

To keep this from happening to you, you must place a limit or stop order with your broker to keep your losses under control. You can even place a trailing stop order so you could specify the amount of loss you can tolerate.

You can stop your losses manually if you do not want to place a stop order. To do this, you have to monitor the price of your investments on a daily basis. When the price of the stock starts to go down, place a sell market order with your broker.

To win consistently in stock trading, you have to keep your losses as low as possible.

Strategy 4

Invest in a Company That Pay Dividends

Many "stock trading for beginners" books will tell you to choose a company that pays dividends. And that's good advice. More often than not, dividend payment is an indication that a company is doing great financially. Plus, it's a good source of regular income, too. Who doesn't want to receive checks in the mail every quarter?

However, you must remember that the company can stop dividend payments anytime. Companies that pay dividends usually have a slow growth rate because they are not reinvesting their profits in expansion.

Strategy 5

Non-Correlated Assets

If you want to become a successful investor, it isn't enough to diversify your assets. It's also wise to invest in non-correlated assets.

Let's look at Tony and Noel's story to illustrate this point. They are both new investors, and they decided to diversify their portfolio and invest in different stocks.

Tony invested his money in different social networking companies. Noel, on the other hand, decided to take diversification to the next level. He invested in non-correlated companies. He invested a little bit of his money in tech companies, but he also invested a little bit in mining, the food industry, and the oil industry.

After a few years, the social networking industry slowed down and Tony ended up losing most of his money. Noel also invested in social networking companies, but he's still doing great because his investments are spread out across different industries.

EXAMPLE OF NON-CORRELATED ASSETS
Gold Company vs Oil Company
Social Media Company vs Gold Company
Oil Company vs Real Estate

Investing in non-correlated stocks reduces risk. It also helps you maximize your profit. For example, if you invest all your money in luxury bag companies, you'll lose a lot of money if that crashes.

Strategy 6

Tax Considerations

It's great to invest in a taxable brokerage account because it has no limits. Naturally, it's taxable. However, so to save money, it's also a good idea to invest in a tax-advantaged account.

The 401(k) plan, for example, is a tax-deferred account. This means that you don't have to pay taxes for your contributions upfront. You can pay the taxes when you reach your retirement age. At that point, you're already in a lower tax bracket. This will save you a lot of money.

Roth IRA is another tax-advantaged plan. You have to pay taxes for your Roth contributions, but when you reach your retirement age and you decide to withdraw the money, you will get a tax refund. It's basically tax-free.

So, even if you have a taxable brokerage account, it's still best to invest in a retirement account, so you can take advantage of its tax benefits.

Strategy 7

Rebalancing and Asset Allocation

As mentioned earlier, do not put all your eggs in one basket. This means that you should not only invest in stocks; you should also invest in other securities, such as bonds.
So, before you start building your portfolio, you have to decide how to allocate your investment fund. Do you want 50% of your investment fund to go to bonds and the rest to stocks?

Let's say that you decide to go with 50-50 asset allocation, but your stocks performed well during the last years, so you decided to sell some of your bonds and buy more stocks. Your asset allocation may shift to 70 (stocks) – 30 (bonds).

When this happens, you must rebalance your asset allocation. You can sell some of your stocks and buy more bonds. This strategy can help reduce your losses if there's a stock market crash.

Strategy 8

Keep your Cost at a Minimum

When you have a tax brokerage account, remember that you have to pay transaction and commission fees per trade. Long-term investment can help you save on transaction fees.

Let's say that you bought one Company S stock for $100. Instead of selling your stock and then buying it back when the price goes up or down, just let it sit in your account. Aim for long-term profits instead. This way, you'll earn more capital appreciation profit, plus you'll save on transaction fees.

Don't be afraid to mix and match different investment strategies so you can earn optimal profits and minimize your investment costs and losses.

And lastly, don't hold on to your stocks forever. Long-term investment is good, but you should sell your stocks if the price is no longer trending up. This can keep you from losing more money.

When a stock's price starts to decline, sell it while its current price is still higher than your purchase price. This way, you'll still earn an investment profit.

Chapter 10 Summary

You'll eventually build a huge investment portfolio as you get better at stock trading and stock market investing.

You must use portfolio management strategies to grow your wealth and your investment portfolio.

Do not make an investment decision based on emotions. Use your brain, not your heart.

Diversify your investments. Invest in different stocks and other securities. If you can afford to buy a real estate property, do that also. Diversifying your investments helps to reduce risk.

Stop your losses by placing stop orders. This will help limit your losses. You can also do this manually. Sell your stocks when you notice that the price is going down.

Invest in companies that pay dividends. This could be a great source of income. Plus, companies that pay dividends are usually stable.

Don't hold on to your stocks for too long. Long-term stock investment is good, but sell your stocks when the time is right.

Take advantage of accounts that come with tax benefits. These accounts can save you a lot of money and they're easy to maintain, too.

Glossary

401k Plan

The 401(k) plan is an employer-sponsored retirement fund. The employee agrees to place a percentage of his/her income into the fund, and the employer matches every dollar the employee saves.

All-or-None Orders

An all-or-none order, or AON, is an order that must be executed in its entirety or not executed at all. For example, if you place an order to buy 1,000 shares of Company X at $5 per share, the broker cannot execute the order if there are only 500 shares available.

Annuities

An annuity is an investment whereby payments/deposits are made at equal intervals. Regular monthly deposits to a savings account and monthly insurance payments are examples of annuities.

Bear Market

This is a condition when investors are so pessimistic that they end up selling their stocks. This decreases the demand for stocks.

Bonds

A bond is a financial security that represents a company's debt. Bonds are used by municipalities, states, governments, and companies to raise funds. Investors earn money from bonds through interest.

Black Swan

Years ago, people believed that all swans are white—until they saw a black swan.
In finance and investment, a black swan is an event that has not occurred in the past, so it's difficult to predict.

A black swan has three characteristics:
- It's unpredictable.
- It has a massive impact on the stock market or the economy.
- You can only identify a black swan after it happened.

Investors should watch out for black swans, as these events often lead to either great investment opportunities or profound losses.

There are a number of black swans that have appeared in the past, including the invention of the internet, the crash of overvalued internet companies from 2000 to 2002, the 2008 financial crisis, the 9/11 attacks, and Brexit.

Bracketed Orders

A bracketed order is designed to limit loss. It can lock in profits by bracketing an order with a trailing stop, a profit target, or a stop loss.

Bracketed orders have an automated exit strategy. Once your desired condition is met, an order is created to exit the position.

Bracketed orders are efficient because they are automated. They're also flexible. You can add a bracket to your whole position or just a part of it. You're not required to put a bracket on all of your shares.

Brokerage Account

A brokerage account is an investment account that you can open through a licensed brokerage firm. After you've deposited money into that account, you can start buying securities like stocks, mutual funds, and bonds.

Brokerage Trade Confirmation

The brokerage trade confirmation is a document that you will receive when you start buying and selling stocks through your brokerage account.

Bull Market

This is a condition when investors are so optimistic that they aggressively purchase stocks. This increases the demand for stocks vis-à-vis its supply.

Buy to Cover Orders

This is a buy order that's used to close out a short position. It is often used in short selling. As the name suggests, this buy order is made to cover a short position or return the stocks borrowed during a short sale.

Capitalization

Capitalization is the sum of a company's stock, long-term debt, and earnings.

Cash Brokerage Account

A cash account is a type of brokerage account in which the investor is required to pay all the securities purchased in full. Investors are usually given two days to make full payment of the stocks they purchased.

Common Stock

A common stock represents ownership of a company. Common stockholders have voting rights on company policies and other matters. It's a risky investment because common stockholders are usually at the bottom of the payout hierarchy. This means that if a company is liquidated, they'll only get their share after the creditors and preferred stockholders are paid.

Compounding

Compounding is the process in which an asset's earnings, from either capital gains or interest, are reinvested to generate additional earnings over time. This growth, calculated using exponential functions, occurs because the investment will generate earnings from both its initial principal and the accumulated earnings from preceding periods. Compounding, therefore, differs from linear growth, where only the principal earns interest each period.

Cyclical Industry

This is an industry that's sensitive to the economic cycles. The companies belonging to these industries have high revenues when the economy is good and have incredibly low revenues when the economy is bad.

Day Trading

This is a stock investment strategy that involves buying and selling stocks within the same day.

GTC Orders

GTC means "good until canceled". This order will expire if unfulfilled at a certain date. It usually expires within thirty to sixty days.

Debt/Equity Ratio

The debt to equity ratio is a metric used to measure a company's financial health.
It is calculated by dividing the company's debt by its equity. When a company has a debt equity ratio of 0.5, it means that the company has a debt of fifty cents for every dollar of equity.

Derivatives

Derivatives are financial securities. Their value is derived from a specific asset or a basket of assets, such as interest rates, market indices, currencies, commodities, bonds, and stocks.

Direct Stock Purchase Plan

This investment plan allows you to purchase stocks directly from the issuing company. You don't have to go through a broker.

Dividend Investing

This strategy involves buying stocks with dividend payments.

Dividend Reinvestment Plan

The dividend reinvestment plan, or DRIP, is an investment plan that allows current shareholders the option of reinvesting their dividend earnings.

The shares purchased through DRIP come from the company's reserve and they're not traded through the stock exchanges. So, trades made through DRIP are commission-free. Plus, most stocks purchased through DRIP are discounted.

Dividend Yield

Dividend yield is the ratio of a corporation's yearly dividend compared to its stock price. It's usually a percentage. To calculate it, you have to divide the company's annual dividend by its share price.

Yearly Dividend ÷ Stock Price = Dividend Yield

Dow Jones Industrial Average (DJIA)

The Dow Jones Industrial Average (or simply the Dow) is a stock market index. It is a sample of thirty companies that are big enough to represent the industry they're in. These companies include IBM, Goldman Sachs, Coca-Cola, Home Depot, Intel, Verizon, Visa, McDonald's, Nike, and Pfizer.

Earnings per Share (EPS)

Earnings-per-share is one of the most popular measurements of a company's profitability. It is the company's net income divided by the number of outstanding shares. The company's EPS is positive if it's earning profits.

ECN or Electronic Communication Network

ECN is a computerized system where people could trade stocks and other securities. This system is commonly used by Foreign Exchange (FOREX) traders.

ETF

Exchange-Traded Fund or ETF is a basket of financial assets that trades like a common stock.

Equity

This is the difference between a company's assets and liabilities. Let's say that Company H has total assets of $100,000, but it has debts worth $20,000. So, its owner equity is $80,000 ($100,000 – $20,000).

Euronext

Euronext is the biggest stock exchange in Europe. It is the product of the merger of the Paris, Brussels, and Amsterdam stock exchanges. It also merged with various stock exchanges, including the New York Stock Exchange.

Fractional Share

A fractional share is less than a "full share." It's the result of a stock split. For example, if an Apple stock costs $40, you can buy a ¼ fractional share for $10.

FINRA

FINRA, or the Financial Industry Regulatory Authority, is a regulatory organization that governs and regulates businesses, dealers, brokers, and other financial professionals. They administer exams and licensing.

Growth Investing

This investment strategy is focused on market capitalization. Growth investors invest in companies that they expect to grow exponentially over time.

Index

An index is a statistical sample that measures the overall health of an industry or a stock market. Investors use indices to make informed and wise decisions.

Index Fund

An index fund is a mutual fund with a stock portfolio that tracks a certain stock market index like the S&P's 500. This investment type has wide market exposure, and it's usually inexpensive.

Initial Public Offering or IPO

It's the process companies go through when they offer their shares to the public for the first time. It's also called "going public".

IRA

IRA or Individual Retirement Account is a tax-advantaged investment account that allows you to save for retirement.

Limit Orders

A limit order is an order to buy or sell a stock at a specific price. A sell limit order is often executed when the stock reaches its limit price. For example, you can instruct your broker to sell a stock you own once its price reaches $50.

A buy limit order is executed when the stock reaches the limit price (or lower). For example, you can ask your broker to buy a company's stock once it goes down to $10 or lower.

Macro-Economic Analysis

This analyzes the behavior, performance, and structure of the economy as a whole. It usually covers an economy's gross domestic product (GDP), unemployment, and policies. It also examines inflation, deflation, the "law of supply and demand," and economic forces.

Margin of Safety

The safety margin is the percentage difference between the current stock price and the intrinsic stock price. To calculate it, you need to use the below formula:

Margin of Safety = Current Stock Price/ Intrinsic Stock Price

A stock with a high margin of safety can give you a higher investment profit because its current stock price is significantly lower than its intrinsic stock price.

Market Cap (Market Capitalization)

Market capitalization or market cap is the total market value (in dollars) of a corporation's outstanding stocks. It measures the company's worth on the market.

Market cap reflects how much investors are willing to pay for a company's stock. So, it's used to speculate a company's future value.

Market Orders

A market order is either a "buy or sell" order that has to be executed immediately at the current market price.

Margin Brokerage Account

A margin account is a type of brokerage account that allows investors to borrow money from their brokers to pay for their purchased stocks. The purchased stocks serve as the collateral for the loan.

Micro-Economics Analysis

This analyzes the behavior of individuals and companies, helping investors pick the right stocks and make wise investment decisions.

Mutual Funds

A mutual fund is a pool of money collected from various individual investors. This is invested in different types of securities, such as stocks and bonds. It's best for people who want to diversify their investments. A financial professional manages this fund.

Nasdaq Composite Index

This is an index based on the capitalization of over 3,300 stocks listed on the Nasdaq stock exchange.

National Association of Securities Dealers Automated Quotations (Nasdaq)

Nasdaq is a stock exchange located in Broadway, New York City. It is the second-largest stock exchange in the world (in terms of the capital it generates).

New York Stock Exchange (NYSE)

The New York Stock Exchange is the biggest stock market in the world (in terms of capitalization). It is located on the iconic Wall Street.

Option

An option is a contract that gives the recipient the right (but not the obligation) to either buy or sell a known asset at a known price at a pre-defined time.

Let's say that Nina and Joey have an agreement. Nina has a car and Joey asks her to give him the right to buy her car for $20,000 in sixty days. Nina agrees not to sell the car to anyone in a month and Bill pays her a 2%, or $400, reservation fee.

Joey doesn't have to buy the car, but he has the option to do so. In this example, Bill is the option buyer or the option holder. Nina is the option seller or option writer.

Option Trading

Option trading is the act of selling or buying options.

OTC Market

This is a decentralized market where trades are usually done through dealers. OTC markets are loosely regulated and less transparent than exchanges.

Outstanding Shares

Outstanding shares are the stocks that a company has already issued to investors. It's the sum of a corporation's common stock, preferred stock, and treasury stock.

PEG Ratio

PEG Ratio or "Price/Earnings to Growth" ratio is used to determine a stock's possible true value. It is computed as:

Peg Ratio = Price-To-Earnings/Annual EPS Growth

A low PEG ratio means that the stock is most likely undervalued. Stocks with a high PEG ratio are most likely overvalued.

Penny Stocks

Penny stocks are stocks that are traded for less than $5. Most penny stocks do not trade on major stock exchanges. These stocks are highly volatile, so it's best for investors who have a high-risk tolerance.

P/E Ratio

The P/E Ratio is the price per share divided by the earnings per share. If the P/E ratio is high, it means that investors are willing to pay more for every $1 of a company's earnings. Stocks with a high P/E ratio have better growth potential, but this doesn't mean that a high P/E ratio is always better. After all, these stocks may just be overvalued.

Preferred Stock

A preferred share is a stock that acts like a bond. It usually comes with dividend payouts, and it's more expensive than common stocks. Preferred stockholders do not have voting rights. But, in case the company sells its assets, they must be paid in full first before common stockholders get their share.

Profit Margin

A profit margin is calculated as:

$$\text{Profit Margin} = (\text{Revenue} - \text{Expenses}) / \text{Revenue}$$

Companies with high-profit margins tend to have tremendous brand loyalty, which allows them to charge a high price for their products. They're also renowned for keeping their expenses under control, while companies with low-profit margins have expense management issues.

Recession

In economics, recession is defined by a significant decrease in economic activity.

Robo-advisor

Robo-advisors are online/digital financial advisors. They manage investors' accounts with minimal human intervention. They can automatically build a diversified portfolio for you.

S&P 500

The Standard & Poor's 500 is an American stock index based on the capitalizations of 500 companies listed on NASDAQ and the New York Stock Exchange.

Security

Security is a financial or paper asset that can be traded. There are many types of securities, including bonds, banknotes, stocks, futures, swaps, debentures, and futures.

Security Exchange Commission

The Security Exchange Commission (or SEC) is a federal agency that enforces the United States securities laws.

Short Selling

This is the sale of a stock that a seller has borrowed. This is the exact reverse of "buy low, sell high."

Stock

A stock or a share is a security. It represents a unit of ownership of a company. It is also an investment vehicle. Many investors buy and sell stocks to grow their money.

Stock Exchange

A stock exchange is where investors buy and sell shares.

Stock Market

A stock market is a place where people buy and sell stocks and other securities. Its purpose is to help companies raise money for their business and to give investors the opportunity to grow their money through stock investment.

Stock Position

This is the amount of a particular stock or security held by an entity or a person.

Stop Order

A stop order (also known as a stop-loss order) is an order to sell or buy a stock once it reaches a specific price called the stop price. This strategy is used to minimize losses, and it's an effective investment risk management technique.

Stop Price

A stop price is a price that generates a market order. Once a stock reaches the stop price, a limit order is created.

Structured Product

A structured product is a pre-packaged investment. It can be a single share or a basket of investment products, such as stocks, derivatives, currencies, and commodities.

Tax Advantage

Tax-advantage is an economic incentive that's associated with certain investment accounts.

Tax-Advantaged

Tax-advantaged accounts are investments that come with tax benefits. These accounts are either tax-deferred or completely tax-free. There are a number of tax-advantaged investments, such as retirement plans and municipal bonds.

Tax Brokerage Account

This investment account doesn't have any tax benefits.

Tax-Deferred

Tax-deferred accounts are investment accounts on which taxes are paid at a future date. There are a number of tax-deferred investments, such as traditional IRAs, 401(k) accounts, 403(b) plans, 457 plans, whole life insurance, variable annuities, and Roth IRAs.

Ticker Symbol

This is an abbreviation of the company's name. This is used to represent the company in the stock market.

Trailing Stop Orders

A trailing stop order is an order to either buy or sell a stock if it moves in a damaging and unfavorable direction. This order automatically adjusts to the most current stock price. A trailing stop order helps the investor increase his profits and limits his losses.

Value Investing

Value investing is an investment strategy whereby you choose a stock that trades below its book value. Value investors invest in stocks that are undervalued.

Conclusion

I'd like to thank and congratulate you for transiting my lines from start to finish. I hope that you've enjoyed this "stock trading for beginners" course. I hope that this book was able to help you start your journey as a stock market investor.

Stock market investing is a great way to grow your wealth and earn more money. Moreover, it's a fun and exhilarating experience. It strengthens your logic and significantly increases your analytical skills. It also allows you to earn passive income.

But before you start your journey to great wealth and financial independence, let's review the major points of this book:

Stock market investing is one of the best ways to build your wealth. It's also a good way to earn passive income.

A stock represents part ownership of a company. When you own a few stocks of a company, you're essentially a partial owner.

Companies create stocks to help raise money for business expansion. When a company is built, it's classified as private, but once it starts selling its shares in the stock market, it's classified as public.

An IPO, or initial public offering, is the process that companies go through when they sell their shares in a stock market for the first time. It's also called "going public."

A stock market is a place where companies issue stocks and where investors buy company shares. A stock exchange is a stock market.

A stock market has two parts—the primary and the secondary market.

There are various stock market players, including the investors, shareholders, listed companies, stockbrokers, venture capitalists, the investment bank, floor trader, floor broker, analysts, and clearinghouses.

You can make money in the stock market in two ways—capital appreciation and dividend payments.

There are two types of stocks—preferred and common.

Common stocks are cheaper, but their holders are at the bottom of the payout hierarchy. This means that common stockholders are only paid after the bondholders and preferred stockholders get their share.

Preferred stocks are rarer and more expensive, but preferred stockholders do not have voting rights. They cannot decide on the company's policies.

Stock prices fluctuate for many reasons, including market volatility, imbalance of the stock's supply and demand, economic policy changes, interest rate changes, economic predictions, inflation, deflation, and natural disasters.

An index is a metric that's used to measure the overall performance of the stock market.

The stock market is heavily affected by speculation. This is the reason why the bull and bear markets exist.

A bull market happens when investors are so optimistic that they end up buying a lot of stocks. This drives the stock prices up.

A bear market happens when investors are pessimistic and sell their stocks accordingly. This decreases the stock prices and can lead to a stock market crash like what happened in 2008.

To invest in stocks, you need to first understand the difference between a stock and a mutual fund. An individual stock represents part ownership of a certain company. A mutual fund, on the other hand, is a basket made of different stocks. An ETF is a mutual fund that's traded in the stock market as a stock.

You must also identify your investing style. Do you want to be a long-term investor or a day trader? This will help you pick the right investment plan.

You must set a budget. How much are you willing to invest in stocks?

Choose a trustworthy brokerage firm to work with. You also need to look at commission and transaction fees. You would want to avoid companies that charge hefty fees.

A 401(k) plan is a retirement plan that comes with an employer matching plan. This means that both the employee and his employer can deposit money into his 401k account.

An IRA, or individual retirement account, is also a retirement plan that comes with tax advantages. There are various types of IRAs—traditional, SIMPLE, Roth, spousal, SEP, and non-deductible.

A taxable brokerage account, as the name suggests, is an investment plan opened through a broker. It doesn't have tax advantages, but it doesn't have limits either, and you can withdraw at any time.

When you have a brokerage account, your broker will execute your trade orders. You don't have to do much.

If you don't want to work with a broker, it's best to open a direct purchase plan. This allows you to purchase the stocks directly from the company.

A dividend reinvestment plan allows you to use your dividend earnings to buy new stocks. This helps you increase your portfolio and investment earnings over time.

There are different investment strategies, including value investing, growth investing, and dividend investing.

Dividend investing is best for those who want to receive dividend checks every quarter. But, keep in mind that dividend payments are not guaranteed. The company can reduce or completely cut dividend payments when profits decrease.

Value investing is for people who want to invest in undervalued and stable companies. Many seasoned investors use this strategy. This is a low-risk strategy, but it can cause you to lose opportunities too.

Growth investing is great for more adventurous and risk-averse investors. Growth investors place their bets on fast-rising companies called "unicorns." This strategy can help you earn thousands of dollars in capital appreciation profit each year. But, it's also risky because most overhyped companies can't live up to all the hype.

Day trading involves buying and selling stock throughout the course of the same day in hopes of earning quick money. It capitalizes on stock market volatility. This strategy is great for full-time traders because it requires a lot of time.

Short-selling is a strategy that doesn't require an upfront investment. It's also a great strategy for those who are a bit pessimistic. This strategy helps you profit from declining prices. When you short sell, you borrow a stock from your broker and sell it at prevailing market price. Once the price goes down, you can buy back the stock and return it to your broker. The difference between your selling price and buying price is your profit.

Before you invest, you must set goals. How much do you want to earn in a year or in a five-year period? How much risk can you take?

To make sure that you pick the right stock, you have to look at various factors, such as the company's financial health, debt/equity ratio, P/E ratio, profitability, market share, and dividend payments.

Look at the company's P/E and PEG ratios to see if it is overvalued.

There are various trades that you can place with your broker, including market orders, limit orders, stop orders, stop-limit orders, and trailing stop orders.

The market order is the most basic of all the order types and it has to be executed within the day. However, if you want to "buy low, sell high," you must do the limit order. This order type allows you to either buy or sell a stock at a specific price during a specific timeframe.

A day order is an order that expires at the end of the trading day.

A stock exchange usually closes at 4:00 P.M, but keep in mind that you can still trade after hours online. You can trade from 4:15 P.M. to 8 P.M, and you can also trade from 8:00 A.M. to 9:15 A.M. before the stock exchange opens.

You can use a stop order to help reduce your loss.

You can always cancel an order. You just have to log in to your account, go to your order, and click on "cancel."

A brokerage account allows you to buy and sell stocks in the stock market. It is usually opened through a broker. This account can hold different types of securities, such as stocks, mutual funds, bonds, ETFs, REITs, and certificates of deposit.

Study your broker's statement carefully to spot fraudulent activities.

You will receive a trade confirmation each time you buy or sell a stock. You must examine your trade confirmation carefully to make sure that your broker executed your order according to your instructions.

You must invest in a company with huge profits and low debt. This is the reason why you should look at the balance sheet carefully.

Review your brokerage confirmation to see if there are errors. Call your broker right away if you see irregularities.

Do not invest all your money right away. Test the water first. Invest a small part of your investment fund, and then, once you earn at least 2% capital appreciation profit, invest another small percentage of your investment fund. Repeat this process until you've invested all the money in your brokerage account.

Before you buy a stock, you must do extensive research. You must do microeconomic analysis and look at the industry as a whole. Is the industry doing well? Is the economy good? Is it a good time to invest in stocks?

After you do your macroeconomic analysis, you should do company research as well. You should check how the company is doing. Is it in good financial health? Is it earning profits?

To maximize your investment profits, you must manage your portfolio well. One way to do this is to diversify your investments.

Index fund investing is one of the best ways to diversify your portfolio. It's inexpensive too.

Invest in non-correlated assets. Investing in non-correlated stocks helps reduce risk and spread your wealth to various industries.

Look at the facts and the numbers. Use logic when making investment decisions. But sometimes, you have to listen to your gut, too. If something doesn't feel right, just don't do it.

Do not invest in just one industry. You never know what will happen. An entire industry may be irrelevant years from now. Remember when CD replaced VHS? Well, Netflix may push cable into extinction soon.

Try to place a stop order with your broker to minimize your losses.

Invest in companies that pay dividends. This is a great way to earn a regular income from your investments.

Do not hold on to your investments for so long. Once the price starts to go down, it's time to let your stocks go. Sometimes, investors get too attached to their stock position that they end up losing profits.

Stock market investment is a complicated animal. You're not going to master it in just a few weeks. Expect to make mistakes or make bad investment decisions. When you do, don't beat yourself up. Mistakes are part of your journey. Just keep going.

Remember that stock market investing is not some "get rich quick" scheme, so you have to be really patient.

And lastly, don't stop learning. Keep reading new materials. Connect with other stock traders and attend seminars. This book is just a beginner's course. There's more to learn.

I wish you the best of luck!

Please Kindly Review This Book

If you have found any value from reading this book, please kindly post a review letting us know about it. It'll only take a minute of your time. Thank you so much!

Printed in Great Britain
by Amazon